UNIVERSITY OF GLASGOW
PRESS

FINANCIAL REPORTING AND ACCOUNTING STANDARDS

Financial Reporting and Accounting Standards

Conference Papers

UNIVERSITY OF GLASGOW
PRESS
1978

ISBN 0 85261 150 1

The Johnstone Smith Chair of Accountancy was instituted in the University of Glasgow in 1925 and the first appointment was made from 1 October 1926. A Conference to mark fifty years of the study of accountancy was held in the University on 28 April 1977. The theme of the Conference was

Financial Reporting and Accounting Standards

The Papers presented at the Conference and an outline of the history of the development of accountancy in the University have been brought together in this book.

Contents

Foreword

THE theme for the Conference to mark fifty years of study of accountancy was chosen as fitting for the occasion. Research in the history of financial reporting would disclose the considerable progress which has been made over the last 125 years, at a greater pace over the last 50 years and, perhaps, even the last 15 years in particular. There are, however, no grounds for complacency. It is always possible in retrospect to know what could have been done better or to complain that progress could have been faster. Perhaps it could. The politics and the mechanics of the process of change make an interesting study — and there could never be a more important time for an understanding of this process in relation to financial reporting.

There are two aspects of progress in financial reporting. Both require academic study and understanding — and both require the understanding of practitioners. There is the conception of the objective and the ideal, the perfect theoretical solution, the ideal model to convey perfect information for optimal decisions. That is a very proper academic proposition. There is the equally proper academic enquiry into the sociological, behavioural and technical constraints on achieving perfection. The academic world, while properly preoccupied with the first of these — the model — has perhaps given insufficient attention to the second — the constraints; perhaps it is a question of resources because the number of those capable of academic research and leadership is still small. The practitioners, preoccupied with urgent and present operational difficulties, pressures and constraints, and at least until recently, failing to give attention to or to understand the nature of the issues involved in change or in the conception of the theoretical ideal, have not universally shown the interest in the development of these academic propositions that a dynamic and forward-looking profession might be expected to do and must do.

The position is, however, changing and the issues involved are now the subject of much greater study by all the parties concerned.

The authors of the Papers are each distinguished by the contributions they have made to better understanding. It would be difficult to assemble a more authoritative team. I doubt if it has been done before. I am sure that this is the right place and that this is the right occasion. I am even more convinced that this is the right time.

In the United States, Senate Sub-Committees have recently recommended greater federal control of the accountancy profession and greater SEC prescription of uniform accounting principles and auditing standards. Not many weeks ago a headline in *The Times* read 'Are accounts too serious to be left to the accountants?' At the present time in the United Kingdom, the authority of the professional bodies in setting the standards of practice in financial reporting is being seriously tested, not least in the move away from historical cost accounting. This is, however, only one aspect of a very much larger issue. What really are the objectives of financial reporting? How can they be achieved? Where does the responsibility lie? These are the questions to which the Papers are addressed. I am certain that those who read them will be stimulated to think again about the real issues and will be assisted towards finding satisfactory answers.

University of Glasgow
April 1977

DAVID FLINT

Fifty Years of Accountancy in the University of Glasgow 1926-1976

by

DAVID FLINT*

In the course of the Conference Proceedings, Professor Flint, the Conference Chairman, outlined the history of the development of accountancy in the University. The following has been extracted from his addresses.

IN A University which has a reputation for distinguished scholarship extending over 526 years, there is a danger that to acclaim a mere 50 years' achievement might be thought to be presumptuous. So, with proper scholarly detachment, we remark on the passing of the years but recognise them as a mere moment in time. Age of itself has no particular merit and fifty years' experience may be no more than one year's experience repeated fifty times. Fifty years, in relation to the human span, is however, a reasonably long period and even in an academic society there is a need from time to time to stand back to consider what has been achieved and in what direction further and future efforts should be made.

The review goes back to an earlier date since it happens that the fiftieth anniversary of the introduction of accountancy studies to the University coincides with the seventy-fifth anniversary of consideration of the introduction of this branch of studies.

In a joint report by the General Council's Committees on Educational Policy and Methods and Finance and Statistics dated 18 March 1901, appointed to consider what part the University might play in promoting commercial education, the Joint Committee applied themselves to considering 'in what way the University might be of service in increasing the number and efficiency of those who were to occupy the chief positions in large commercial undertakings'.

While the Joint Committee reported that they would welcome the granting by the Senate of special recognition to graduates who had certain practical experience and who showed a competent knowledge of the higher phases of commercial science and practice, they found that 'successful business men speak of the solid advantages of the Arts course, and they do not consider

* Professor Flint occupies a Chair of Accountancy in the University of Glasgow

the existing regulations for the Master of Arts Degree so narrow as to justify the suggestion of a new Degree'; and they did not recommend that the University should make provision for instruction in such subjects as 'the complete practice of accountancy', rejecting at the same time 'the organisation of factories and offices' and 'the principles of Trades Unions, Trusts and combines'.

The committee's remit was continued.

The matter of a faculty of commerce or a degree in commerce was thereafter a subject of exchanges between the General Council and the Court for the next twenty-five years. According to the record, the initiative came from the General Council and was dealt with by the Court by the time honoured expedient of referring the matter to a committee. Such a committee was appointed by the Court in 1903. A report from the General Council in 1905 was referred to that committee and a further report from the General Council was again referred to it in 1906. Nothing appears to have happened.

As a result of a report from the General Council in 1911, the Court appointed an advisory committee which managed to report some three years later, in July 1914. The Court approved of the report, having come to the conclusion that it was not expedient to take steps for the establishment of a faculty of commerce or the institution of a special degree in commerce.

The General Council returned to the subject in 1917, anxious that the University should have some scheme ready to put into operation as soon as peace was restored. The Court consulted with the Commercial College but was still not disposed to do anything.

In 1918, however, the General Council once again made representations to the Court and an advisory committee on education for commerce was set up with representatives of the Commercial College and the Chamber of Commerce as well as the University. I have found no record of its reporting or advising on the matter.

It would be interesting to be able to learn more of the basis of the concern of the General Council on the one hand and of the continuing reluctance of the Court on the other. This, I am sure, would have something to tell us, not only about the approach to education for the accountancy profession, but of education for commerce and industry in general in this country.

It is clear that the existence of worthwhile classes in commercial subjects at the Glasgow Athenaeum Commercial College had some bearing on the views taken. The General Council gave consideration to the availability of the Commercial College class for University purposes and there was some discussion of a postgraduate diploma in commerce for Arts graduates—the classes to be taken at the Commercial College. The Chairman of the Commercial College who was also a leading chartered accountant in Glasgow and a forceful personality, must, I think, be presumed to have had a considerable influence at that time. In a memorandum to the committee of the General Council he expressed the view that a number of commercial subjects, including accounting, could not yet be taught at a degree standard, and that they should be dealt with in a Commercial College — although his view is partly based on the difficulty of finding teachers who would deal with the subject on a university level.

The Advisory Committees set up by the Court in 1911 and 1918 included representatives from the Commercial College with which it was obviously thought necessary to keep in close consultation.

Although a faculty of commerce or a degree in commerce was a matter of some periodic enquiry, the subject of accountancy lay over until 1925 when David Johnstone Smith, President of The Institute of Accountants and Actuaries in Glasgow, 1922–24, offered a sum for the endowment of a Chair of Accountancy in the University, 'not only in the interests of the profession but for the benefit of a great commercial community such as Glasgow', which, fortunately for the accountancy profession in Scotland, ensured the place of accountancy in the University and resulted in successive generations of Glasgow chartered accountants passing through the University. This has done much to create the intellectual basis of the accountancy profession in Scotland and has had a very much wider influence, since many of the accountants educated and trained in Scotland have moved further afield, to London and overseas. David Johnstone Smith, by his benefaction, created the opportunity for the academic development of accountancy in the University of Glasgow — which thus acquired the fourth Chair in the United Kingdom, being predated only by Birmingham, London, and Edinburgh — and for the close cooperation between the universities and the practical world of accounting. This cooperation, based on the mutual trust and respect of academics and practitioners, is vital to the professions.

Court, Senate and General Council were all pleased to accept the gift of the endowment and there followed some discussion on the tenure of the appointment and on the question of cooperation with the Commercial College.

The General Council agreed that 'the principles and practice of accountancy may be considered a subject worthy of research and study and not alien to the purposes of a university' although they cautioned it was 'unlikely to become a subject of general culture'. Commenting on the draft ordinance for the institution of the Johnstone Smith Chair of Accountancy, however, they regretted that there was no suggestion of cooperation with the College in connection with the new Chair, and they took the view that 'it was difficult to see how full use of the Chair can be made apart from the students who are under training at the Commercial College'.* The point that the professor should, in addition to his University duties, be under an obligation to give instruction to students in the Commercial College was apparently put

* This last reservation was in due course partly dealt with by the requirement of the Glasgow Institute that the C.A. apprentices should transfer their attendance from the College to the University.

to Mr. Johnstone Smith who had agreed the terms of the draft ordinance. This would not have been an innovation for the University since the recently created Chairs of Italian and Spanish had included a responsibility for teaching at the Commercial College and, incidently, were on a five year tenure. Mr. Johnstone Smith was not prepared, however, to concede the point as he believed it would make the duties of the professor too burdensome and preclude his continued engagement in practice, which he and his advisers regarded as important.

The other matter of substance on the draft ordinance was the length of tenure which was proposed to be twelve years. The Senate raised objection to the limitation to twelve years; on the other hand, the General Council were doubtful of the wisdom of fixing the period at twelve, suggesting five might be preferable (after the precedent of Spanish and Italian). On this also Johnstone Smith was adamant, offering to the Senate a compromise at fifteen years if this would be helpful.

I do not know if the Chair was advertised or applications sought. I have found no records. There is, however, deposited in the archives, a letter to the Principal signed by the President of The Institute of Accountants and Actuaries in Glasgow, the immediate Past President, and by David Johnstone Smith, recommending John Loudon as outstandingly suitable for appointment, and John Loudon was duly appointed first Professor in the Johnstone Smith Chair from 1 October 1926.

A course in accountancy within the graduating curriculum for the degrees in law was introduced from that date and although the syllabus has substantially changed, that course subsists to the present day. There was also a non-graduating course in accountancy introduced for the benefit of apprentices of The Institute of Accountants and Actuaries in Glasgow. They were already required by the entrance regulations to attend a course in Scots Law at the University and were now required to take the University class in accountancy in place of one which had previously been provided at the Commercial College, previously the Glasgow Athenaeum Commercial College.

These requirements, together with attendance at a University course in economics, continued until 1973–74 when the 'academic year' for C.A. apprentices was discontinued, the entry requirement being then raised to a relevant qualifying degree.

The last twelve years have seen a dramatic expansion of the study of accountancy in the University in the shape of the introduction of advanced and honours study and the extension of the ordinary classes in 1965; the introduction of the specialist degrees of Bachelor of Accountancy and Master of Accountancy in 1968, and of the graduate Diploma in Accountancy in 1974; the development of the financial aspects of management studies as that branch of study in the University also grew; and the creation of two Chairs of Accountancy, additional to the Johnstone Smith Chair, in 1973 and 1975.

From 1926, instruction in taxation was undertaken by the Professor of Accountancy and this formed part of the syllabus of the courses until 1965 when a separate course within the LL.B. curriculum was introduced. With the introduction of the B.Acc. degree in 1968, advanced and honours courses in taxation were offered and by 1975 the subject of study was so well established in its own right that Faculty, Senate and Court readily responded to a proposal from the Professor of Accountancy that taxation be recognised as a separate department of study for all the purposes of the University.

There are now now three professors, three senior lecturers and six lecturers in post, a well established curriculum of undergraduate courses to honours level, and a steady flow of well qualified graduates to the several branches of the accountancy profession. Research and graduate study have perforce played a minor role during a period of considerable undergraduate expansion and it is, therefore, in these areas that the emphasis of new effort now lies.

An Academic Viewpoint

by

PETER E. M. STANDISH

I FINANCIAL REPORTING IN THE ECONOMIC AND POLITICAL MARKET PLACES

THE objective of this contribution to the Conference is to identify or reinterpret the function of corporate financial reporting in the operating context of private business enterprise at this time, especially in Britain. Analysis of the effectiveness of financial reporting and of steps required for its development are usually based on value judgements that a flourishing business sector is preferable to a languishing one, and that financial reporting is effective to the extent it contributes to that result. Those value judgements underlie this discussion also, though it is possible to view the financial reporting process analytically, without regard to the merits of the ends it is intended to serve, and that will to some extent be attempted in the discussion also.

1 Information and the communication network as variables in resource allocation

Information utility theory directs attention to what determines the value of information in the hands of those wishing or likely to take decisions for which it is relevant. A number of attributes of information apparently affect its utility,[1] especially informativeness, relevance, timeliness and accuracy. Their significance can be assessed in terms of effect on capacity of information to convey news, i.e. to apprise its user of relationships and context which he would otherwise be without.

Informativeness refers to the array or extent of data available from a particular source, e.g. the collection of financial statements and related explanation in an annual report.

Relevance refers to the extent to which a user perceives some set of data as appropriate input to his intended decision process.

Timeliness refers to the extent to which a set of data is available to the user sufficiently often or with sufficient rapidity that it possesses relevance.

Accuracy refers to the extent to which a set of data corresponds with the phenomena it represents, having regard to the attributes being represented and the system for taking and evaluating observations of that attribute.

For purposes of evaluating information utility, let it be assumed that the utility of particular information and of the communication network for distributing it can only be assessed by reference to:

(i) the user's prior familiarity with comparable information;
(ii) his location in the distribution network;
(iii) his access to other related sets of data (whether or not from the same source).

Admission of this assumption means that there is no generally optimal set of reported financial information or related communication network since the utility of any particular set of data or of arrangements for its distribution depend on the user's prior experience with comparable data, the means by which he obtains it and the total array of data available to him.

The effectiveness of present arrangements for financial reporting and the probable effect of proposals for change cannot be properly understood without recognition and analysis of the interdependence of those factors. Figure 1 directs attention to variables in the total information-decision system of resource allocation, where the specific set of variables relating to formal periodic financial reports are seen to be but one of many strands reaching the various user groups. For purposes of illustration, another explicit formal strand connects forecast macro data (e.g. public statistical data on demographic trends, planned capital expenditure, etc.) to user groups, and a broken line represents an implicit, informal strand by which company forecasts for managerial purposes nevertheless are transmitted to certain user groups (e.g. as data made available to a banker or as inside information leaked to external users).

Those whose aspirations run to general systems theory and application would perhaps wish to attempt a grand design for an information network which maximises benefits available to all information users.[2] Those who doubt the worthwhileness of such a venture will probably be content to concentrate attention on the operation and apparent utility effects of particular strands in the network. Nevertheless, even in this latter case, the diagram underscores the need to consider existing or possible alternate strands which may be more cost effective or, which amounts to the same thing, provide greater utility (to users, or jointly to business enterprises and users).

2 Financial information and periodic reporting as resource allocation variables in the market

The capital market

The term is used here to refer to the set of agents who allocate capital resources according to expectations of risk and return. Periodic financial reporting is believed particularly to be relevant to and used by capital

Figure 1 : Financial information — communication network

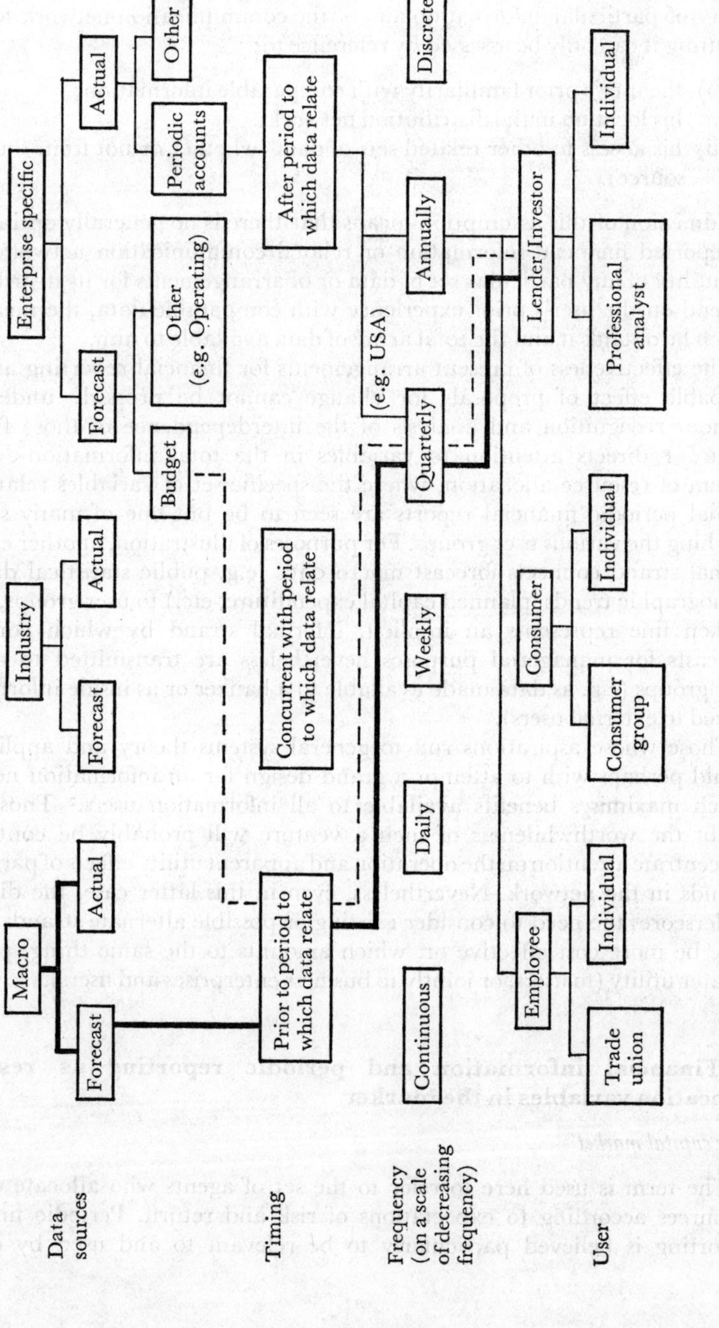

The three connecting rules, bold, faint and broken, denote three separate communication networks.

market agents in arriving at their allocation decisions. Moreover, evidence indicates that stock market prices, which in effect impound agents' decisions, show significantly positive correlation with values of some regularly reported performance indicators, e.g. earnings per share.[3]

Assume that business enterprises which report information to the market and agents in the market both act as if securities are priced by reference to expected future cash flows discounted for systematic risk and the required market rate of return.[4] Assume further that companies wish to maximise the value placed by the market on expected cash flows to be generated from future operations.[5] In that case, companies wish to communicate financial information at times and in a manner consistent with that objective. In the absence of constraints and penalties, and in the absence of alternative information networks, this can be achieved within a given time horizon by:

(i) Deliberate misrepresentation of those performance indicators thought likely to influence agents.

(ii) Classification of performance indicators on a basis which represents certain components of performance as transient or as self-cancelling over time, other components as stable or with growth characteristics.[6] For example, if a company believes that stable, growing earnings will enhance its share price, it would wish to represent significant deviations from the serial trend in earnings as extraordinary, i.e. non-recurring.

The means by which a company may seek to influence valuation of expected cash flows depends partly on the extent to which any particular form of reporting is constrained by externally imposed rules and standards, and partly by its perception of which strands in the communication network connecting it to users are of greatest interest to them. Thus, periodic financial reporting may be contsrained so much that a company is left with no effective discretion to vary reported information in either of the foregoing ways. Or, if companies perceived that agents are able by means of alternate data sources to evaluate cash flows on the basis of information available prior to the periodic report, it would be reasonable for them to regard reporting more as a matter of form than of important substance.

From the viewpoint of the capital market agent, attention must centre on identifying those data sources and communication strands which provide the earliest delivery of information likely to lead to changes in risk and return assessment, since he cannot expect to achieve above average returns from information already available to the market.[7] Since financial reports appear well after the interval to which they relate and the events to which they refer are already known in various ways to many people (employees, auditors, suppliers, major customers, etc.), it is likely that much of their message has already been anticipated.[8] Reported financial information has, however, several general characteristics of interest:

(i) The underlying accounting process seeks to measure performance in terms of a common attribute, viz. money or money-equivalent amounts. This contrasts with the variety of operational measures gathered by and available at earlier points in time to various parties of interest (e.g. data on product volumes, numbers of employees, etc.).
(ii) The balance sheet, profit and loss account and other associated financial statements are uniquely the product of the central accounting concept of duality[9] and associated data collection and processing. They offer an integrated, synoptic view of the business not otherwise available.
(iii) Verification procedures applied to statutory accounts and notes raise the apparent level of accuracy of financial data (though not necessarily the level of relevance, which is for the user to assess rather than the provider of data).

These characteristics support the view that financial reports convey information of kinds or of an accuracy not available by other means. In Part II, suggestions are made for extending the range of reported data, on the ground that the potential utility of periodic reporting is not fully exploited at present. If that is to be more than an exercise in mere assertion, however, it is necessary to establish criteria for assessing utility of reported information. To do so requires, in the light of the foregoing discussion of the communication network, attention to these issues:

(i) The relative advantages of providing all agents with the same set of published accounts of a particular company (e.g. the annual report and accounts) or with the possibility of agents making a choice between different sets of data.
(ii) The relationship between scale and frequency of user decisions, and needs for information, especially in regard to timing, frequency and extent of detail.
(iii) The meaning of accuracy in financial information and the ability of users to distinguish factual data from interpretative comment.

Subsequent discussion will address these issues.

The Political Market

This term is used to refer to the process whereby political policies are established in relation to the role of private business enterprise in society, the attitude of government toward business, and the distribution of social wealth. Whilst the roles of the capital and political markets are not mutually exclusive, it is assumed in this discussion that the capital market is primarily concerned with wealth creation, as a means for rewarding risk investment, whereas the political market is primarily concerned with deciding and applying criteria for wealth distribution.

At this time the interdependence between financial reporting and the evolution of political criteria for wealth distribution have more than abstract interest, given the existence and strength of sharply diverse views on the subject. By contrast with a laissez-faire view that wealth distribution should be determined by the operation of the capital market, without the need for supervention of political criteria and public policies on the subject, we currently can see the following views strongly advanced (whether singly or in combination):

(i) Private business enterprise should totally or in designated sectors be squeezed out of existence, with ownership and control transferred to the state (or proxies for the state, e.g. worker co-operatives).
(ii) The investment, financing and profitability of business should be closely regulated and, as required, capital resources be supplied by the public sector (e.g. from taxation revenue, or public borrowing). A corollary to this objective is that achievement of profitable operation is not necessary and, possibly, is socially undesirable since it distributes wealth to investors (even if the investor is the state) and away from other groups (e.g. consumers, employees).

In this situation, what would be regarded in the capital market as a desirable financial result (e.g. increased earnings per share) may be regarded as undesirable in the political market. As political attitudes give vent to public policies which impinge on business cash flows and profitability, they will form part of the data relevant to the capital market and will affect return-risk assessment. In this way, political objectives and evaluations spill over into the capital market, becoming in effect its objectives and evaluations. In the process, however, as can be seen in Britain, risk investment is sharply reduced because political constraints prevent its being adequately rewarded and a number of undesirable social and economic consequences follow.

It does not seem worthwhile trying to consider what financial information about business enterprise should be reported to those who wish to eradicate that enterprise. Though accounting of some kind is needed even in highly centralist socialist economies, it is notable that there is little or no public financial reporting and that the practice of accounting seems enfeebled, from a professional viewpoint.[10]

Instead, assume that financial reporting is required in the political market-place to assist decisions intended to maximise social utility through creation and distribution of enterprise income. So that financial reporting may be effective for this purpose, the issues stated earlier in relation to the capital market need to be reinterpreted in relation to the political market, viz:

(i) The need to identify those institutions or classes or persons to whom financial information is potentially relevant for purposes of formulating public policy, and to assess modes of reporting appropriate to their decisions.

(ii) The relationship between scale and frequency of political user decisions and needs for information.
(iii) Criteria for accuracy and materiality of information used in a political context.

As with the capital market, subsequent discussion will address these issues.

II BACK TO SQUARE ONE

1 Discovering the factual basis of financial performance accounting

Earlier use of the term 'accounting' was primarily concerned with counting up or with a reckoning of a money quantity and transactions in money. Though these meanings are still important and describe much of accounting process, it is common to speak of accounting as financial measurement, where this process refers to quantitative estimation of a conceptual magnitude such as profit, asset value, net worth. The king in his counting house counting up his money is able to make factual assertions about the magnitude of money tokens, but if he wishes to determine his wealth or income, a set of measurement objectives and bases will need to be specified. Because those central financial concepts are purely abstract, it does not seem satisfactory to regard measurements of their quantity as yielding factual information, even though the information can be verified on criteria such as consensus or reasonableness.

Those abstract representations are, however, derived in part from various factual states and experiences, the relationship between the representations and factual basis being determined according to prevailing accounting standards. Figure 2 sets out the more important factual items commonly accounted for and the nature of the abstract financial representations made about them. In brief, the money amounts of transactions and the objects and rights acquired or disposed can be factually accounted for; derived assertions about their value, and of periodic income and wealth cannot.

The extent of financial interpretation underlying reported data derives from a number of factors, principally:

(i) Legal requirements and constraints, e.g. the prohibition against paying dividends from capital, which requires an interpretative distinction to be made between income and capital.
(ii) Non-statutory explicit financial standards, e.g. relating to stock valuation, or determination of profit on contract work in progress.
(iii) Implicit financial standards, reflecting a degree of consensus about financial measurement objectives in a particular community, e.g. the emphasis in German accounting on conservatism and associated writing down of asset values.
(iv) Individual accounting policies of the enterprise, formulated in the absence of statutory or professional requirements, e.g. the policy

Figure 2: Factual transactions and financial representations

Factual event or state	Classification conditional on expected outcome	Financial representation
Cash income	Sales to customers	Allocated periodic sales revenue
	Realisation of capital assets	Capital gains/loss
	Issue of securities, mortgages, etc.	{Paid capital {Debts payable
Cash expenditure	Operations	Allocated periodic costs
	Purchase of capital assets	Cost of capital assets
	Repayment of capital, loans, etc.	Reduction of paid capital, debts payable
Unpaid contractual debts	Receivable/payable	Value of receivables/payable
	Not receivable	Written off
Physical amounts of tangible assets, owned or being acquired:		
Stocks	Cost recoverable	Cost or value
	Cost not recoverable	Market value
Fixed assets	Cost recoverable	Depreciated cost/value
Investments	Cost below market	Cost or value
	Cost above market	Market value
Physical amounts of leased assets	(Capital leases	Capitalised
	(Operating leases	Not capitalised
—	Capitalised expenditures for intangibles	R & D goodwill, etc.
—	Unrealised gains/losses	Movements in reserves and retained earnings

followed over some years by Rolls-Royce Ltd. in capitalising substantial amounts of aero engine development costs.

Interpretative material provided by an enterprise creates an overlay on events, which itself has to be interpreted by the user. Frequently it obscures or supplants factual data, e.g. the relationship between recognised earnings and operating cash flows which often has to be deduced by the user. In situations where alternative accounting rules or standards exist, some are likely to result in a closer correspondence between factual events or states and their interpretation, than others. For example, translation at current rates of the historic foreign currency cost of fixed assets results in recognition of the unrealised effects of exchange rate changes subsequent to the time of their acquisition. Whether or not those unrealised effects correspond with operating cash flows, either in the same foreign currency or not, is an issue which could only be determined by reference to suitably classified cash flow data.

The significance to the user of the interpretative reporting practices followed by an enterprise is influenced by these factors:

(i) Accounting standards adopted by the profession are in the domain of public knowledge and therefore users can be presumed to be aware of them and their general effects on reported performance. For example, if the proposed British current cost accounting standard comes into effect, users would need to understand that value estimates would generally be substituted for historic costs of non-monetary assets.[11]

(ii) The precise effect of known standards is often difficult to estimate. For example, without knowledge of the cost, age or type of fixed asset being revalued, an external user cannot effectively estimate the extent of recognised realisable gain or loss resulting from revaluation.

(iii) Many known standards permit internal choice of accounting method. For example, standards on stock valuation allow a wide variety of choices concerning basis of cost association with sales (FIFO, LIFO, etc.) and treatment of overheads. The ability of the user to interpret the effect of the general standard depends on information being given about the combination of choices made by the enterprise.

(iv) In the event of there being no known standard to be applied to some aspect of reporting, or if the enterprise chooses a procedure different from the known standard, the user can only assess the significance of interpretative material if information is provided about the procedure used.

(v) The set of standards and practices optionally chosen by the enterprise for reporting purposes may give insights into managerial style and expectations about the future.[12] For example, companies wishing to report earnings growth on long-term projects would prefer rules which result in early recognition of earnings.

2 The parameters of financial performance

A potent source of confusion in the present design of accounting standards and in user assessment of reported financial information is a lack of clear agreement about the objectives of financial measurement and reporting.[13] Consider the following possibilities:

(i) Emphasis on factual events, with explicit reporting of relevant items (cf. Figure 2), e.g. classified cash receipts and expenditures, amounts payable and receivable, physical quantities of major operating assets.
(ii) Emphasis on valuation of wealth and measurement of income as a derivative of wealth estimates.
(iii) Restriction of reported information to data concerned with events over a past period of time.
(iv) Extension of reported information to estimate of events over a future period of time.

Conventional reporting, based on what is rather loosely termed historic cost accounting, has been principally confined to a subset of factual events of a past period of time, but has also usually included a discretionary coverage of possible future events, e.g. in accounting for contingencies, and capitalisation of intangible expenditures on the implied assumption of their recoverability from future revenues. Proposals for current cost accounting likewise would nominally deal with events of a past period of time, though it can be shown that the valuation processes which current cost accounting requires are derivatives of expectations about future events.[14] Thus, not only is there disagreement about reporting objectives, but reported data, whether actual or proposed, does not necessarily correspond with any particular objective.[15]

Resolution of these difficulties is only possible if we identify more clearly and agree upon the boundaries or parameters of financial performance and the associated field of activities to be observed and accounted for. Assuming that all classes of financial information users are interested in the viability of the enterprise, as a system for providing a future benefit or stream of benefits (e.g. wages, dividends, products, purchase orders), it follows that users have a common interest in enterprise ability to create additional valuable resources, as denoted by its expected future net operating cash inflows. As noted earlier, capital asset pricing theory provides a model for valuing those expected cash flows. Though there is a dearth of comparable explanatory theory for the valuation of future benefits to an employee, or consumer, it can be seen that the possibility of benefits being realised depends similarly on the enterprise's cash flow generating ability.[16]

Recognition of the primary importance of cash flow generation directs attention to the determinants of cash flows. For any enterprise, cash flows result from a mix of constraints and variables reflecting:

(i) macro factors, e.g. economic, social, political, environmental, applicable to societies in which the enterprise operates.
(ii) industry factors, e.g. changes in technology.
(iii) factors specific to the enterprise, e.g. its unique input/output relationships.

We cannot, however, definitely identify or quantify all those factors which in the past significantly affected cash flows, because of the extent of their interdependence and the fact that, even to careful observers within the enterprise, many outcomes result from imperfectly specified systems in the nature of a 'black box'.

Nevertheless, the management of an enterprise is or ought to be better placed than any other group to identify significant past influences on cash flows during the reporting period and probable future influences. Though information about macro and industry factors is for the most part in the domain of public knowledge, it is often difficult for those external to an enterprise to assess how it has been or may be affected by changes in external factors. For example, a change in anti-pollution regulations will differentially affect business cash flows according to their activity mix and the extent to which their operations currently diverge from requirements.

Whilst users of accounting information make their own final assessments of performance and prospects of the enterprise, the relevance of financial reporting to their needs will be strengthened as the enterprise is able to identify and report data concerned with cash flows and the factors which affect them. It is not clear that much of the recent thrust of developments in accounting standards has been assisting that cause, presumably because its importance has not been fully recognized. The remainder of this Part considers ways in which that could be done.

3 The rationale for accrual accounting and allocation

If the original distinguishing feature of accounting methodology was the concept of duality, the neat major feature was the advent of accrual accounting and the third was that of allocation, as interest grew in cost analysis for control purposes. The latter two are interpretative concepts which underpin present practices of cost and revenue matching by time periods and by activities. Exposure to them and training in their use is such an important part of the acquisition of accounting skills that accountants perhaps fail to realise or remember the extent to which accrual and allocation are employed, nor do they seem to reflect on why they use these concepts.

An example is seen in the practice of deferred tax accounting. This is founded on the view that income tax is a cost and as such should be matched against revenues on a periodic basis. It thus represents a logical extension of accounting concepts and practices in other areas of financial measurement. The cumulative result of deferred tax accounting is, however, recognition of a liability which seems to have a very contingent quality but an alarming propensity for growth relative to other liabilities and equities. If there is no credible likelihood of deferred tax liabilities being realised or reversed, the user naturally wonders what object is to be served by the procedure.[17]

In assessing the utility of alternate bases of measurement, it is important to consider whether and to what extent consequent measures can be derived from each other. For example, the conventional procedures of fund flow analysis enable crude measures of fund or cash flows to be derived from balance sheets and the income statement. Since this is an exercise in reclassification of published data, it literally cannot add to available information. If the earnings series and the operating fund or cash flow series are uncorrelated, however, it is possible that one will provide greater insights than the other for purposes of estimating future performance.

In that sense, any and every basis for estimating earnings and profitability may appear useful, on the offchance that they may provide additional insights.[18] That argument pays no regard, however, to accounting costs nor does it provide a credible rationale for accrual accounting and allocation. At present, the case for employing these concepts seems rather tattered. Some accrual practices seem over-elaborate and artificial; others perhaps are employed in an attempt to smooth out earnings fluctuations or to stave off the day of cost recognition. Allocation of joint input costs and of fixed costs over time periods, practices which are pervasive through financial accounting, is an arbitrary process and can be used to produce widely differing results.[19] Oftentimes they seem to be employed in a mechanistic way (e.g. straightline depreciation) without any particular interpretative significance. If these criticisms are accepted, there is an urgent need to rethink the objectives of the relevant accounting procedures and the interpretability of performance measures derived by extensive accrual and allocation.

4 Entity multi-dimensional performance as the essential focus of reporting

Many of the shortcomings of financial reporting and the difficulties users appear to have in interpreting it are traceable to an unimaginative and over-zealous effort by the accounting profession to employ its central concepts of duality, accrual and allocation. The procrustean bed of double entry and of formalised financial statements is not necessarily, however, the most effective or direct way for the enterprise to alert users to the existence of factors which have influenced or may be likely to influence cash flows. For example, tax allocation and the creation of a deferred tax provision may alert the user to the possibility that the rate of actual tax payments in the future could be higher than currently, due to a reversal of timing differences. But the same points could be more directly and clearly explained by information showing taxable income (where significant, by countries of operation), tax paid and estimated to be payable on taxable income, and the extent to which the enterprise has availed itself of timing differences (on depreciation, etc.) as a means for reducing taxable income. In addition, the possibility of capital gains taxes arising on realisation of gains (e.g. of revalued fixed assets) can be directly noted and quantified if it were significant for purposes of drawing attention to contingent factors affecting cash flows.

Similarly, we can see that adoption of proposals for current cost accounting are neither necessary nor efficient as a way of drawing attention to the estimated effect of inflation on cash flows, given the subjectivity of current value estimates. Instead of incorporating current values into balance sheet and profit and loss account, which has the effect of further obscuring the factual basis of the accounts, the enterprise can directly draw attention to and comment on issues such as:

(i) Possible future cash flow repercussions of rising replacement costs, changing technology and market demand.
(ii) The nature and effect of any public policy constraints on pricing, target rate of return and dividend distribution.

The essence of the argument is that accounts as currently presented are being made to carry too many messages of differing significance or probability of occurrence. At the same time, reporting practices and accounting standards have not adequately been concerned with reporting the enterprise's assessment of factors influencing cash flows. To deal with this, it would be better to restrict the financial statements entirely or as closely as possible to factual information about cash flows, commitments and, for the purposes of arriving at distributable net operating cash inflows, the actual money amounts of non-monetary assets not yet recovered from charges for use or sales of assets.

To address the problem of reporting critical determinants of cash flows and providing information about them requires recognition of the points at which reporting departs from factual data to interpretation. Interpretative information need not, and on prior argument effectively cannot, be integrated into the conventional framework of duality and interrelated financial statements. Moreover, it should not be accorded the same status as factual accounting data, especially in relation to audit verification. It is no more reasonable to expect auditors to attest the truth and fairness of assertions about the estimated effect of changing technology on production costs than it would be to expect attestation about the causes of the Great War. Any factual events which are the subject of interpretation can, however, presumably be verified. And even in relation to interpretative data it is feasible to establish guidelines or requirements for the types of items to be reported.

Figure 3 sets out a possible list of potential determinants of cash flows, on which information could be offered (subject to materiality in the affairs of the enterprise). It is intended to capture the multi-dimensional performance of the entity, but seen ultimately from the viewpoint of actual or potential

Figure 3: Cash flows of the enterprise

1. Actual flows of the period, classified by currencies of major operation

Operating receipts:
Sales revenue (net of change in debtors)
Financial receipts (interest, dividends)

Operating payments:
Costs of operations (net of changes in creditors)
Financial payments (interest, dividends)
Income and withholding taxes

Capital receipts:
Capital stock issued for cash
Loans received
Sales of non-trading assets

Capital expenditures:
Acquisition of non-trading assets
Loans granted

2. Events of the period with expected effects on cash flows, classified by countries of major effect

Arising from operations and capital programmes:
Incomplete sales orders and purchases commitments
Implemented technological changes leading to changes in input/output relationships
Introduction of new or substantially modified products
Commissioning and closure of facilities

Changes in regulatory requirements and constraints, relating to:
Environmental and technical factors
Consumer safeguards
Employment conditions
Price and investment controls
Tax and dividend distribution
Currency exchange controls

Relevant price movements, applicable to the enterprise:
Commodities
Labour
Services
Financing costs
Capital equipment

cash flow effects as proxies for ability to deliver particular kinds of benefits.[20] Reporting developed along these lines offers the prospect of a clearer distinction between factual events and interpretation. At the same time, the enterprise would be in the position of commenting directly on factors relevant to its affairs (both internal to operations and arising externally), without recourse to elaborate accounting contrivances.

III REINVENTING THE WHEEL: MULTI-NATIONAL DETERMINATION OF ACCOUNTING STANDARDS

1 Why have accounting standards?

Accounting standards may be regarded as fulfilling various functions, not all of them necessarily consistent or compatible with each other:

(i) As a means for relieving uncertainty, whereby accountants can refer to statements of standards for guidance or direction in the selection and use of accounting concepts and procedures. In that event, the accountant can avoid the necessity for having to deal with each or any task from what he conceives to be first principles. Statements of standards thus represent a codification of collective professional experience or of requirements imposed or accountants with the object of determining their future experience.

(ii) As a means for indicating to users the accounting concepts and techniques which they may expect to have been employed by accountants, except where an enterprise or its auditors indicate otherwise. The existence of standards then relieves users' uncertainty about a number of the characteristics of reported information and reduces the extent of explanation which would otherwise be necessary (or at least desirable) by enterprises about their mode of accounting.

(iii) As a means for regulating accounting practices and financial reporting. In Britain, for example, there seems to be a tacit agreement that the accounting profession has primary responsibility for determining the way in which statutory financial disclosure requirements are to be accounted for, in terms of measurement bases, classification of items in published accounts and explanatory comment by companies. It is noteworthy, however, that the way in which it discharges this task comes to assume a regulatory role, as auditors are expected to judge the truth and fairness of reported accounts in terms of their compliance with accounting standards. A (the?) next step would be to require that those responsible for accounting within the enterprise adhere to professional statements of standards for purposes of drawing up enterprise financial statements.

(iv) As a means for recording and identifying information about accepted

> accounting procedures. In recent years, there has been a pronounced tendency toward development of standards which, in relation to particular subjects, reduce or eliminate accounting alternatives in favour of some preferred method or a small number of methods. Even so, standards constitute a record of accepted concepts and practices and, depending on their wording, may also record rejected or discarded concepts and practices. They thus provide a useful data base or repository for tracing the evolution of financial reporting.[21]

Nevertheless, the case for statements of accounting standards, as the system has evolved in the major English-speaking countries, needs reexamination. No other profession seeks to control or delimit the substantive professional exercise of judgement in this way. Doctors, engineers, educators are not bound by nor can they even refer to codified professional statements for the purposes of deciding how to treat health problems, designs and operate interactive production processes, or designing and operating educational programmes.

In those cases and in the other professions generally, the practitioner who seeks guidance in the analysis of issues and in responding to problems can only turn to the relevant common body of ideas, factual knowledge and procedures, received through professional training and available in the literature of emerging research findings. The discipline of accounting also has a common body of ideas, factual knowledge and procedures (recorded in numerous standard textbooks) and a vigorous research literature.

Thus although the operation of each profession is *sui generis*, we should ask why the accounting profession requires this singular apparatus of standards and standard setting and, if possible, compare its cost to the benefits derived by users or with costs of alternative possibilities for communicating financial information. For this purpose consider the British three tier financial reporting system applicable to companies:

(i) The Companies Acts require a display of periodic financial information, some of the requirements being highly specific (e.g. disclosure of paid capital, by classes), but the remainder being indicative (e.g. assets classified under headings appropriate to the business). Their requirements constitute a minimum disclosure standard for companies to follow.

(ii) Statements of accounting standards, concerned with bases of valuation and measurement (e.g. stock valuation) and to some extent with display of information (e.g. extraordinary items).[22]

(iii) Optional additional disclosure by companies.[23]

Note that none of these sets out standards on methods of accounting, data collection and processing, for which the practitioner turns, analogous with other professions, to the received body of knowledge and research.

The case for imposing statutory disclosure requirements rests on the judgement that:

(i) Depending on the extent to which they are specific rather than indicative, they call for a standardised array of data which assists comparisons between time periods and enterprises.[24]

(ii) Through requirements relating to regularity and timing of reports, statutory disclosure improves the publicly available flow of information and reduces opportunities for trading on inside information. However, the effectiveness of statutory disclosure has been little studied either from the viewpoint of comparing requirements in different countries or jurisdictions,[25] or in terms of identifying and applying criteria for an improved set of disclosure requirements.[26]

Statements of accounting standards, which constitute the second tier of the reporting system, are overwhelmingly directed to the provision of interpretative information, e.g. estimation of non-monetary asset values, allocation of fixed or joint costs to time periods (e.g. depreciation) or activities (e.g. overheads), and analysis of components of profitability such as holdings gains and operating profit. The quest for developing acceptable accounting standards dealing with such issues has proved expensive (in money terms), frequently acrimonious and, in terms of accomplished improvements in utility of reported data, inconclusive or frustrating.[27] A current example of all these difficulties is afforded by the twists and turns of the British accounting profession to establish and then disestablish deferred tax accounting, a practice for which there never has been an observable demand by interest groups (e.g. analysts) and which appears to have had little or no perceptible effect on user decisions (e.g. pricing of securities by reference to the extent of deferred tax charges or provisions).[28]

It is time for us, in considering the objectives of accounting standard setting and its likely utility, to recognise more clearly the nature of the process. Consider the possibilities, bearing in mind the functions of accounting standards outlined above:

(i) As a process of discovering a set of basic postulates from which are to be derived by deductive analysis more detailed operational standards forming a coherent and internally consistent whole.

Individual theoreticians and the accounting profession have been and continue to be attracted to this view of how the standard setting process should operate and continue to search for or to elaborate deductive frameworks of proposal for accounting and reporting.[29] This view of the process, however, only has validity if we can develop a very powerful systems theory of reporting such that the decision process of all classes of users is known, that the accounting information having greatest utility to users is known, that the cost of providing the information is known and that it would be possible to apply a Pareto optimal criterion of utility to cost-benefit analysis of reporting.[30] In the absence of these conditions, it follows that there is no strong method for demonstrating the superiority of grounds for preferring one deductive model of accounting and reporting over another.[31] The history of evolution of deductive models and reactions to them suggests that this process is an important one (being an instance of the epistemological importance of deductive theory building), but is not sufficient by itself, especially when there are urgent time constraints on arriving at accepted standards.

(ii) As a process of political bargaining between the various interest groups, in which each seeks to maximise its own utility with respect to costs and benefits of providing and using accounting information.

Carried to extremes, acceptance of this view of the standard setting process would justify dispensing altogether with the search for deductive accounting and reporting models, except in so far as any particular interest group believes that effort spent in that direction is justified in terms of a likely increase in its own utility. For example, analysts may believe that the utility of reported information could be improved if information were to correspond more closely with the requirements of capital asset pricing theory in an efficient capital market context. They must then, in an open political bargaining system, persuade preparers that information for analytical purposes can be provided at no greater cost to companies, e.g. in actual outlays for operating the accounting system, or in terms of adverse effects on the perceived riskiness of companies resulting from changed data availability.

The implications of a bargaining system view are important. Just as in political bargaining at the macro-society level, it can be expected that bargaining over reporting standards will generally be stimulated by crisis conditions, associated with major changes in macro-social variables (e.g. the rate of inflation, prevailing political attitudes). The history of accounting standard setting to date has fitted this description,[32] and on this view its future history would follow much the same path. Those who criticise existing accounting standard setting as insufficiently forward looking are probably therefore misunderstanding the efficiency of a process which to them looks untidy and ineffectual, but which is reflecting the relative political strengths and utility maximising objectives of interest groups.

Even if we accept, however, that standard setting is a political bargaining process, largely operating in response to random crises, it is still worthwhile to consider whether improvements are desirable or possible in the institutional process by which bargaining is conducted and bargains are struck. The remainder of this Part is devoted to that issue and to suggestions for its improvement. Since the extent of standards applicable to enterprises generally impinges on the extent to which they may individually develop and apply reporting practices, the question of what should be the relative balance between standardisation and individual discretionary reporting is also considered.

2 If there are to be standards, who should determine them?

This is an issue which becomes relevant and need be seriously addressed only when standard setting is viewed as a political bargaining process. In turn, in an open democratic society, satisfactory operation of that process depends on resulting standards being accepted by interest groups as legitimate. For this to occur, the following are required:

(i) A system for participation by groups having an interest in the outcome of the bargaining process. Without that, the authority of particular standards will be weakened to the extent they are imposed on and conflict with group interests not compromised by bargaining.

(ii) Subordinate to the above, processes whereby interest groups legitimise for the benefit of their members the mode by which they participate in the bargaining process, e.g. by election of representative members, or appointment on the basis of perceived skills.

Referring back to the operations of financial reporting in the capital market and political market (I.1), we see the likelihood of two participatory processes, summarised in Figure 4 and adapted to the probable information needs and decisions of each broad arena. If it is accepted that there is in each case a need for verification as a means for achieving greater information accuracy, then the first three interest groups possibly appear self-evident. Even so, some further points need to be made:

(i) Under present statutory arrangements, directors are responsible for preparation and presentation of the annual accounts. Given the magnitude (and risks) of that responsibility, it seems obvious that they participate in the standard setting process so that it will be sufficiently attuned to constraints on management.

(ii) In practice, much of the selection of accounting policies and procedures, as well as their implementation, falls to financial executives and accountants who frequently have a professional affiliation as well. They therefore are a significant separate group with direct interest in the outcomes of standard setting.

(iii) Capital market agents do not have homogeneous risk preferences or expectations and therefore participation is desirable on a basis which reflects major risk bearing segments of the market, particularly equity investment and debt financing. Since regulation of the capital market is directly concerned with the network by which price sensitive information is communicated by companies to capital market agents, participation by those responsible for its regulation is also desirable.

(iv) In the political market, interest groups are less well identified and so consequently are their decisions and preferences. Nevertheless, as current conditions demonstrate, their attitudes and actions determine the political constraints in which business operates. More precisely,

Figure 4: Participation in financial standard setting

Interest group	Possible representatives
Capital market	
Enterprises	Directors Financial executives/accountants
Verifiers	Auditors
Capital market	Investors Lenders Stock market regulators
Academic	Accounting/finance
Political market	
Enterprises	Directors Financial accountants/ executives Public relations
Verifiers	Auditors: Private sector Public sector
User groups	Consumers Employees Environmentalists
Academic	Political science/public communication Skills related to political market interest groups (e.g. labour relations, environment)
Public regulation	Policy making Administration

the ways in which groups seek to maximise utility through political pressures impose costs and create opportunities for business. Many of their apparent objectives are not directly expressed in monetary terms and could not be accounted for within the basic duality framework of accounting. Hence it is likely that achieving acceptable reporting standards in the political market depends on extending reporting to a wider range of performance indicators than customarily fall within the ambit of enterprise reporting. For example, to communicate effectively the environmental impact of business operations probably requires gathering and transmitting a variety of measures of physical properties and relationships (e.g. gaseous emissions, by types), together with associated interpretative comment.

The organisation and management of the wider data base called for, together with verification of reported information appropriate to this end, may be a function which calls for a wider set of participants in communication, verification and data analysis than are presently involved in standard setting. Accountants and auditors have to date not been greatly involved in reporting to political interest groups and at this stage it is an open question whether their roles should be expanded to embrace responsibility for reporting of the kinds envisaged, or whether other groups with professional communication skills should also accept some degree of responsibility, both for reporting as such and for participation in standard setting.

(v) The extent of government involvement in developing and administering public policy toward business enterprise gives it a particular interest in determining its requirements for data on enterprise operations, including requirements for verification of data. Till now, the business sector has not actively sought to develop standards for reporting data relevant to public policy but usually has confined itself to reacting to legislative requirements for information (or to the prospect of such requirements). Though this may have seemed the best course from the viewpoint of minimising reporting costs and government encroachment on business, the danger is that government, by not being drawn into setting reporting standards, has not been made sufficiently aware of business conditions and the impact of public policy. The self-interest of private enterprise would be better served by a more creative and participatory approach to the problem of communicating with the public sector.[33]

(vi) The academic interest group in both categories of Figure 4 refers to those teachers and researchers engaged in systematic study and analysis of enterprise, from both analytic and prescriptive viewpoints, but who in that capacity do not have a financial interest in the outcomes of enterprise operations. They are the only group with a comparative advantage and likely interest in extended deductive model building and empirical testing of the kind referred to earlier, by contrast with the shorter term sequential problem solving preferences of parties in a bargaining process.

Academic participation in setting reporting standards therefore is desirable as a means for reducing the chance that problems and opportunities effective over a longer time scale will not be overlooked or excessively discounted by self-interest groups seeking to maximise short run utility. For example, financial reporting appropriate to conditions of low inflation has proved grossly inappropriate to high inflation, when holding gains are included in historic cost profits but not matched fully by net cash inflows available for taxation or dividend distribution. This was not adequately foreseen by any of the non-academic interest groups which continued to prefer the higher profits recognised under historic cost accounting. By contrast, the academic group had drawn attention to the inadequacies of historic cost accounting, especially at significant rates of inflation, and advanced a number of accounting models which would modify or replace it.[34] The chances of adopting these or even carrying out necessary experimentation must have been higher if academics had been explicitly involved at an earlier stage in the process of standard setting.

It is beyond the scope of this paper to advance particular schemes for recognising interest groups, for inducing their participation in standard setting, for determining their basis of representation or for creating an effective standard setting institution. As a comparison. Figure 5 shows the composition of the British Accounting Standards Committee and the American Financial Accounting Standards Board, together with the constituencies represented by members of those bodies. They reveal major differences in the interest groups with direct participation in standard setting and provide food for thought to those who argue for changes in existing arrangements.[35]

3 Does every industrial nation need to develop its own standards?

A striking phenomenon of recent years has been the growth in numbers of professional accounting bodies issuing statements of standards, and in the rate at which standards, in various stages of evolution, are being issued. Not surprisingly, the same problems are being addressed in various countries and reflected in multiple standards, in many cases embodying different recommendations. The most notable instance concerns proposals for inflation accounting, which are the subject of proposed or operative standards in a number of countries.[36] Although the canons of historic cost accounting are differently interpreted in different countries, it seems that proposed inflation accounting standards may produce even greater diversity in reported performance.

Do international differences in accounting practices and standards have

Figure 5: Composition of British and American accounting standard setting institutions

Membership of British Accounting Standards Committee

Professional institution	Professional activity:				Total
	Public practice	Financial executive	Public sector	Academic	
ICA England and Wales	7	2	1	1	11
ICA Scotland	2	1	–	–	3
ICA Ireland	2	–	–	–	2
ACA	1	1	–	–	2
ICMA	–	1	–	1	2
CIPFA	–	–	2	–	2
	12	5	3	2	22

Membership of American Financial Accounting Standards Board

AICPA	4	–	–	–	4
(not known)	–	1	1	1	3
	4	1	1	1	7

significant effects on decisions of interest groups, especially decisions for implementation across national boundaries (e.g. investment, lending, co-ordination of national public policies toward business)? This question is a particular instance of the problem of assessing significance of accounting differences for decision purposes generally. Evidence strongly suggests that differences which can be reconciled by reference to alternative data are not significant.[37] For example, users of financial data are likely to be indifferent to whether or not a company capitalises research and development expenditure, provided the extent of capitalised amount is disclosed, since the user can classify the amount as expended or as creating a potentially revenue earning asset according to his evaluation.

To the user, differences create a necessity to seek means for adjusting data of particular enterprises on to a more comparable and relevant basis. If disclosed information is not sufficiently specific concerning bases of financial measurement and the nature or meaning of the various classifications used for reporting purposes, the user may be unaware of the existence or amount of differences. For example, amounts of fixed assets disclosed without an indication of the basis on which they are determined presents the user with data of unknown comparability which can only be adjusted if at all by reference to sources of information beyond the enterprise report, e.g. to any authoritative source which may indicate the relevant accounting standard.

Sufficient disclosure of bases on which amounts are determined and of classification descriptions enables the user who wishes to compare data for different enterprises or time periods to identify where accounting differences exist, even if the means for converting data into comparable form are not directly given. For example, if Company X values stock on a first-in-first-out basis and Company Y on a last-in-first-out basis, the user who wishes to assess their performance in comparable terms must devise some effective procedure for converting them on to a common basis (e.g. both on to FIFO). Analysts are well familiar with many of the means for doing this, either by inference from other reported data (e.g. the rate of stock turnover, as a means for estimating the time lag between FIFO and LIFO) or by reference to data external to the enterprise.[38]

These considerations are important in assessing the significance of international differences for analytic purposes and what, if anything, should be done to harmonise international accounting standards. To users of particular national accounting data not requiring to make decisions across national boundaries, international differences have no effect on data utility and harmonisation of standards would be irrelevant. To users making decisions with effects across boundaries, the most direct solution is for the user to seek data from enterprises which conform to his standard requirements (e.g. as is commonly done by the major international banks for their credit evaluation purposes). In all likelihood, international differences present the greatest difficulty to equity investors, operating at arm's length from enterprises, and confronted by annual and interim financial reports of widely differing types, in terms of range of data, description and classification of items, and accounting policies used by enterprises.

In so far as nations wish to promote international movement of capital resources for investing and lending, accounting differences constitute a cause of friction in processes of disseminating and analysing financial information. How serious the effects may be is impossible to know, though where companies see advantage in adapting their reporting practices to a wider international audience, we may assume they will do so.[39] In the absence of perceived advantage, attempts to impose harmonisation are likely to be expensive of effort and of doubtful success. Differences between industrial nations in their systems of economic and political organisation, in their capital markets, in the stages of development of their accounting professions, are too great for any process of harmonisation to represent more than a fragile papering over incompatible realities. The chances of mitigating adverse effects of accounting differences will be improved if we pursue limited aims and concentrate on essentials.

Two earlier lines of argument may be recalled in this regard:

(i) The factual basis of actual financial performance exists independently of the manner in which it is interpreted for financial reporting purposes.

(ii) Reporting grows in relevance to the extent it clearly conveys information about actual cash flows and observed determinants of past and likely future cash flows.

Applying them to international differences, the most useful line of direction for development is toward reporting a standardised array of data, e.g. in relation to the range of income statement and balance sheet items, reporting of classified cash flows, treatment of subsidiary and associated company operations Where reported performance is derived from or affected by valuation or other interpretative estimates (e.g. stock values dependent on allocated overheads, current valuation of fixed assets), the user needs information about bases of valuation and, as far as possible, a clear demarcation between factual data on cash flows and interpretation.

Within nations, reporting and accounting standards are needed to address the problems caused by diversity in the range of reported information and the tendency which companies exhibit to supplant or obscure factual data by interpretative information which they can more firmly control. Beyond dealing with those issues, the case for issuing formalised standards looks shaky. Between nations the same considerations apply, though if the problems of standardising the range of reported data and of the role of interpretative material are to be tackled, there must be an effective process for exchanging information on national reporting practices and requirements, and for producing a consensus on desirable changes. In practical terms that too can be seen as a political bargaining process translated into an international context, to which the general arguments developed in III.2 are applicable.

4 Guidelines for the development of standards

The development of accounting standards, as we observe that process in a number of countries over recent years, has been neither harmonious nor, in terms of reducing criticism of financial reporting and the accounting profession, particularly fruitful. Perhaps the objective to be sought by these efforts have not been sufficiently well identified or thought through; perhaps the wrong questions have been asked. In this section suggestions are advanced for a fresh view of the subject, based on the main strands of previous argument:

(i) Coordination of reported information.

Financial reporting serves agents in both the capital and political markets. Though it may be appropriate to vary the range, presentation and interpretative information provided for each of these, and for segments of them (e.g. lenders and equity investors; trade unions and environmentalists), the credibility and relevance of reported data will be reduced if the differing sets of reported information are in conflict. If mechanisms for distributing information work efficiently, it is futile for companies to imagine that different messages can be transmitted to different interest groups without those messages spilling over to other groups. For example, it would be ineffective for business to want trade unions to assess business profitability by reference only to current operating profit, but to want the capital market to assess it by the generally greater amount of current operating profit plus holding gains.

(ii) The place of financial information in the reporting network.

Financial communication, whether by periodic reports or by less formal means (e.g. briefing sessions for professional analysts), distributes price sensitive information. In studying the financial reporting process and seeking its improvement, we must understand the actual distribution network; otherwise wasted effort will be spent on devising reporting schemes which are not relevant to users able to obtain access earlier in time to acceptably reliable indicators of performance. For example, some demands for an expanded range of reporting to employees call for data not now systematically made available to the capital market, e.g. capital investment plans, including the commissioning and closure of operating facilities. Are employees to be placed in a more privileged position than capital market agents, in terms of early access to price sensitive information? If so, we can predict that employees will become capital market agents to a greater extent than at present, either by direct market operations or by selling information to analysts, investing institutions, etc.

(iii) Financial information and the total information set available to users.

Financial performance measures reported by the enterprise are to a significant extent anticipated, due to the manner in which the enterprise communication network operates and the availability of relevant data from sources external to the enterprise. For example, although security pricing in the capital market is sensitive to the rate of inflation, the use of procedures for reflecting inflation in company accounts leads to information reaching the capital market well after the market is already aware of inflation (from macro-economic and other news disseminated through the media).

Enterprise data which interprets the effect of external conditions on its operations, where users would find it difficult to estimate that effect, and data which confirm or verify user expectations formed in conditions of significant uncertainty, by definition provide news which is useful. Information which meets neither of these conditions, being available with little error from other sources, should not be a serious candidate for disclosure by individual enterprises.

(iv) Statements of standards as a data base on reporting practices.

Statements of standards are implicitly, and can be organised as, an important data resource whereby users can study the characteristics of reporting in a particular economy. Professional effort to eliminate different interpretative approaches to reporting may be better replaced by effort to record and codify the principal methods used or advocated for interpretative reporting of performance. The very choices made by companies in presenting their interpretations of financial performance provide interesting signals about managerial perception of interrelationships between the enterprise and the environment and likely future cash flow effects. A first line of defence for alerting the user to those choices is through disclosure by the enterprise of what choices were made (e.g. method of depreciation, basis of stock valuation). A second line of defence is through the existence of explanatory standards indicating how these choices are implemented and what their effects are (e.g. that capitalisation of overheads delays cost recognition) The rôle of the auditor, who examines whether managerial accounting policies are explained and consistently carried out, is to provide the bridge between these two safeguards and the information user.

The role of stated accounting standards as a data base in relation to international accounting differences is especially important. In that context many of the homogeneous variables operating in a given economy are absent, e.g. common disclosure and tax laws, established accounting conventions. Information on national accounting practices and standards made available in a form for use and interpretation outside the particular country has grown considerably in recent years, though usually in a fairly condensed, summary form. Systematic comparative study of financial reporting standards their determinants and of communication networks in different countries is much harder to come by.[40]

(v) Evolution of standards by bargaining and consensus.

It can be expected that individuals and even institutions will continue to come forward with grand designs for establishing reporting standards. This is better viewed, however, as an input to ongoing processes of bargaining by conflicting interest groups. If the existence of this process is more realistically accepted and studied, we can then address ourselves to the systems necessary for involving the various groups and establishing the authority of bargaining outcomes.

IV IF I WERE KING . . .

This final part is both a reprise and a personal view of ways in which development of financial reporting and accounting standards in Britain can be made more responsive to user needs and more effective. It is based on the belief that the accounting profession at present acts in partial ignorance of the sources of information available to users and of the network by which information is communicated. As a result the profession has not sufficiently identified the distinctive contribution it can make through financial reporting, and the respects in which it is not particularly able to make an effective contribution. Until that occurs, many of its present concerns will continue to be unproductive and misunderstood by users.

1 Reliance on a well informed capital market

If we accept the ability of the capital market to price securities efficiently (i.e. without persistent bias) on the basis of available information, then the accounting profession need not feel so concerned to lead users by the hand. For example, the repeated arguments about which definition of profit should be highlighted in accounts as the 'bottom line' or all-inclusive measure of distributable earnings seem unnecessary. Provided the principal components of cash flows and interpretative representations of earnings are disclosed, the capital market can be assumed capable of pricing earnings in conjunction with other available data. Since evidence strongly indicates that the market disregards reported contrivances (well-intentioned or otherwise) to affect earnings independently of cash flows there needs to be more emphasis on adequate display of factual data and clearer identification of interpretative material.

Reporting to the political market for purposes of public policy and as an input to the decisions of interest groups in the political arena needs to be seen as an extension of reporting to the capital market, i.e. providing relevant data as input to estimating and evaluating future benefits. Because developments in the political arena affect the capital market, and vice-versa, and because the boundaries between costs borne by enterprise and by other interest groups fluctuate in response to public policy and social attitudes, significant influences on cash flows are wider than company reports often indicate. Enterprises may consider there are short-term advantages from restricting their range of reported information, but the desirability of adequate information being made available to conflicting interest groups points to the evolution of a wider range of performance indicators.

2 Frequency, timing and extent of reporting

These three variables appear highly significant for assessing the relevance of reported information. Yet they have been strangely neglected by the accounting profession in choosing issues of greatest priority for developing statements of standards. Frequency and timing of reports affect the extent to which users seek out alternate data sources and, as a related issue, affect the value of information to users at different points in the communication network. For example the value of inside information is likely to be diminished with more frequent and faster reporting. By increasing the number of variables about which information is provided, we can improve users' ability to assess interrelationships between the enterprise and its environment. All three factors rate more attention than hitherto in the development of accounting standards.

3 The dangers of building walls from the top down

Reliance on an authoritarian or oligarchic process for imposing accounting standards may look attractive, as a means for quelling arguments, but it is stultifying and ineffective, because it inhibits the personal need of accountants and users to acquire greater knowledge and understanding of reporting processes and possibilities. Though Britain has a relatively large accounting profession and one of high ethical standards, educational requirements for admission to the profession are, for the times, surprisingly unsophisticated, compared with most of the other major industrial nations. Speaking collectively of the six British and Irish professional bodies, the profession has not moved to adopt graduate entry requirements nor does it require academic study of accounting and business finance, either as preparation for or subsequent to professional admission The result is that most currently qualified members can only be expected to have an imperfect understanding of contentious reporting issues confronting the profession,[41] more especially for these reasons:

(i) The body of knowledge to which members were exposed at the stage of becoming professionally qualified was almost devoid of a theoretical base or framework, but highly technical and prescriptive in character. Moreover, this material is studied in the context of preparation for professional examinations, not as a part of an exercise to identify accounting objectives and means to attain them.

(ii) Existing professional training and educational arrangements do not put members in contact with or attach any evident importance to the literature of accounting research on deductive and empirical issues. It is highly probable that most members are unaware that this literature exists, let alone that it has potential relevance to their tasks.

4 Maoism and accounting standards

The brief flowering of the Maoist ideal that the one hundred flowers should be let bloom retains its validity for accounting, as for all professions. The spectacle of practitioners waiting for solutions to be promulgated from on high is not heartening, either in terms of their personal professionalism or the likelihood of accounting standards being based on robust understanding. The British profession must take a positive commitment to raising relevant educational standards for entry and for post qualifying development if there is to be a lively flow of ideas and a wider appreciation of the function and effectiveness of accounting. It is probably naive to imagine that the need for formal accounting standards would wither away as intellectual standards are raised, but at least the balance might be swung back in the direction of accepting and requiring the full exercise of individual professional judgement in accounting standards.

NOTES

1. Information utility is the subject of Feltham, 1972. It was also the subject of the AICPA Objectives Study, 1973, and of extensive discussion in FASB, *Discussion Memorandum*, 1976, where a number of different attributes of useful information are discussed; see p. 149 for a tabular summary.

2. A system in which benefit to any user can only be increased by reduction of benefit to another user would be Pareto optimal; see Standish monograph, 1975, Ch. II. 1.

3. Most published work of this kind is based on American data, eg. Beaver, Kettler and Scholes, 1970. An as yet unpublished study on German data is Coenenberg and Brandi, 1976.

4. This amounts to a summary of the two parameter (risk and return) capital asset pricing model, e.g. as elaborated in Jensen, 1972.

5. For example, in according with multi-period financial decision models operating under uncertainty; see Haley and Schall, 1973.

6. The nature of patterns of performance over time, as represented by earnings, and their significance for predicting future earnings growth are examined by Lev, 1974, Ch. 8.

7. The stage at which information is fully reflected in security prices is the subject of much speculation and enquiry. Perhaps the most widely tested and accepted view is the semi-strong form of the efficient market hypothesis which holds that security prices at a given time fully reflect all public information about a company; see Dyckman *et al.*, 1975, Ch. 1.

8. Two well known studies of the extent to which reported earnings have already been anticipated by the market are in Ball and Brown, 1968, and Beaver, 1968. A research project currently in progress at the London Business School (J.R. Franks *et al.*,) is obtaining results showing that security prices adjust rather slowly to instances of reported earnings which are abnormally high or low, relative to expected earnings.

9. i.e. the classificatory concept of asset and equity applied to those items deemed to form part of financial position. For its particular importance and evolution in accounting, see Mattessich, 1964, Chs, 2 and 4.

10. For evidence of the state of the accounting profession in Russia, see Bailey, 1977.

11. Accounting Standards Committee, ED 18, 1976.

12. On accounting practices as an indicator of managerial style, see Sorter *et al.*, 1966; on discretionary classification of extraordinary items, as a means for smoothing normal or sustainable earnings, see Barnea *et al.*, 1976.

13. Evidence that there is no mere hair splitting issue is abundantly provided by the search for objectives in FASB, *Tentative Conclusions*, 1976.

14. See Standish, 1977, for further explanation on this point.

15. The possibility of a gap between objectives and methods is an important issue in the design of the FASB conceptual framework project for gathering information about user needs (see previous FASB references).

16. To this should be added a second order possibility, namely the likelihood of benefits being provided by alternative means (e.g. state support) in the event of business failure. Generally this possibility appears quite low, and failure results in widespread loss of benefit to different parties on interest.

17. The British, but not the American, accounting profession has now conceded this; see Accounting Standards Committee, ED19, 1977.

18. Hence the recurring argument that reports should convey a variety of alternate performance measures, e.g. based on historic cost, constant purchasing power adjustments and current cost (or valuation).

19. This has been strongly demonstrated by Thomas, 1974.

20. This objective was the main concern of Staubus, 1961, an imaginative study of possible ways to provide more effective information to investors.

21. E.g. see Grady, 1965, and APB Accounting Principles, 1973.

22. As contained in the Accounting Standards Committee, *Statements* and *Proposed statements of accounting practice* (the latter issued as Exposure Drafts).

23. For an indication of its range and extent, see The Institute of Chartered Accountants in England and Wales. *Survey of published accounts, 1976* and previous comparable surveys.

24. By comparison with Britain, reporting requirements in some countries are highly standardised, perhaps the most notable example being the French 'Le Plan Compatable' (Beeny, 1976).

25. An interesting comparative study of British and American requirements in terms of regulatory cost and the impact of requirements on the capital market is contained in Benston, 1976.

26. A set of proposals along these lines is developed in Standish, Bulletin, 1975.

27. On the cost of developing standards, see for example Annual Reports of the Financial Accounting Foundation, sponsor of the Financial Accounting Standards Board. In 1976, FASB expenditure was $US 4.0 mill. The travail of developing standards is recorded for some countries in Zeff, 1971.

28. Note especially the empirical results on this question obtained by Beaver and Dukes, 1973.

29. Probably the most extensive deductive framework is in Chambers, 1966. Other examples include Mattessich, 1964; Edwards and Bell, 1961; and Sterling, 1970. There are also professionally sponsored attempts to set out deductive frameworks or at least to identify the issues, notably the FASB Discussion Memorandum, 1976.

30. The unlikelihood of this being even theoretically feasible is examined in Marshall, 1972.

31. Hence arguments for and against the possibility of demonstrating on deductive grounds the general superiority of a normative set of standards, Demski, 1976; Cushing, 1977.

32. Some unpublished work (author not known; to appear in *The Accounting Review*) shows that there has over a substantial time interval been a significant relationship between initial falls in stock market prices and actions by the British and American professions to issue statements of general accounting principles. Stock prices themselves are closely affected by macro-social variables.

33. Public agencies play a role in accounting standard setting in a number of countries, e.g. in USA through the Securities and Exchange Commission, and in Japan through the Business Accounting Deliberation Council, supervised by the Ministry of Finance.

34. Significant work in these directions appeared as far back as Jones, 1956, and Mathews and Grant, 1957.

35. For further analysis of the issues, see Moonitz, 1974.

36. Summarised in International Accounting Standards Committee, 1976.

37. The effect on security prices of accounting differences, especially of announced changes in accounting policies, has been examined in a number of studies, e.g. Ball, 1972.

38. Published studies describing procedures for adjusting reported data by reference to public information include Davidson, Stickney and Weil, 1976, on constant purchasing adjustments, and Falkenstein and Weil, 1977, on replacement value adjustments to historic cost accounts.

39. There are many instances of this in recent years, notably French, German and Japanese companies issuing data adjusted onto the basis of British or American standards, e.g. Compagnie Française des Pétroles; Saint-Gobain-Pont-à-Mousson; BASF Aktiengesellschaft; Mitsubishi Heavy Industries. For evidence on the extent of optimal changes in reporting by European Countries, see Barrett, 1976.

40. Two fairly condensed summaries of European reporting practices are Lafferty, 1975, and Oldham, 1975. A wider, but even more condensed summary is Price Waterhouse, 1975. The Institute of Chartered Accountants in England and Wales is sponsoring publication of a more detailed series of studies of reporting practices in particular European countries, e.g. Beeny, 1976.

41. The consequences of this state of affairs for arriving at a high level of common understanding about the inflation accounting issue is examined in Stamp, 1977.

BIBLIOGRAPHY

Accounting Objectives Study Group, *Objectives of Financial Statements* (American Institute of Certified Public Accountants, October 1973).

Accounting Principles Board, *Accounting Principles — Original Pronouncements* (American Institute of Certified Public Accountants, 1973).

Accounting Standards Committee, *Current cost accounting*, Exposure Draft No. 18 (London: 30 November, 1976).

Accounting Standards Committee, *Accounting for deferred taxation*, Exposure Draft No, 19 (London: 25 May, 1977).

D. T. Bailey, 'The accounting profession in Russia', *Accountancy* (March 1977).

Ray Ball, 'Changes in Accounting Techniques and Stock Prices', *Epirical Research in Accounting: Selected Studies, 1972*, Supplement to *Journal of Accounting Research*.

Ray Ball and Philip Brown, 'An Empirical Evaluation of Accounting Income Numbers, *Journal of Accounting Research* (Autumn 1968).

Amir Barnea, Joshua Ronen and Simcha Sadan, 'Classificatory Smoothing of Income with Extraordinary Items', *The Accounting Review* (January 1976).

M. Edgar Barrett, 'Financial Reporting Practices: Disclosure and Comprehensiveness in an International Setting', *Journal of Accounting Research* (Spring 1976).

William H. Beaver, 'The Information Content of Annual Earnings Announcements', *Empirical Research in Accounting: Selected Studies, 1968*, Supplement to *Journal of Accounting Research*.

William H. Beaver and Roland E. Dukes, 'Interperiod Tax Allocation and δ Depreciation Methods: Some Empirical Results', *The Accounting Review* (July 1973).

William H. Beaver, Paul Kettler and Myron Scholes, 'The Association Between Market Determined and Accounting Determined Risk Measures', *The Accounting Review* (October 1970).

J. H. Beeny, *European Financial Reporting: France* (The Institute of Chartered Accountants in England and Wales, 1976).

George J. Benston, *Corporate financial disclosure in the UK and the USA* (Farnborough, 1976).

Raymond J. Chambers, *Accounting, Evaluation and Economic Behaviour* (Englewood Cliffs, 1966).

A. G. Coenenberg and E. Brandi, 'The Information Content of Annual Accounting Income Numbers of German Corporations — A Review of German Accounting Standards and Some Preliminary Empirical Results', paper presented at the 'Seminar on Accounting in Europe', *Institute for Advanced Studies in Management*, Brussels 1976.

Barry E. Cushing, 'On the Possibility of Optimal Accounting Principles', *The Accounting Review* (April 1977).

Sidney Davidson, Clyde P. Stickney and Roman L. Weil, *Inflation Accounting: A Guide for the Accountant and the Financial Analyst* (New York, 1976).

Joel S. Demski, 'An Economic Analysis of the Chambers' Normative Standard', *The Accounting Review* (July 1976).

Thomas R. Dyckman, David H. Downes and Robert P. Magee, *Efficient Capital Markets And Accounting: A Critical Analysis* (Englewood Cliffs, 1975).

Edgar O. Edwards and Philip W. Bell, *The Theory and Measurement of Business Income* (Berkeley and Los Angeles, 1961).

Angela Falkenstein and Roman L. Weil, 'Replacement Cost Accounting: What Will Income Statements Based on the SEC Disclosures Show? — Part II', *Financial Analysts Journal* (March-April 1977).

Gerald A. Feltham, *Information Evaluation* (American Accounting Association, Studies in Accounting Research, No. 5, 1972).

(a) Financial Accounting Standards Board, *Conceptual Framework for Financial Accounting and Reporting: Elements of Financial Statements and Their Measurement*, Discussion Memorandum (December 2, 1976).

(b) Financial Accounting Standards Board, *Tentative Conclusions on Objectives of Financial Statements*, (December 2, 1976).

Paul Grady, *Inventory of Generally Accepted Accounting Principles for Business Enterprises* (American Institute of Certified Public Accountants, Accounting Research Study No. 7, 1965).

Charles W. Haley and Lawrence D. Schall, *The Theory of Financial Decisions* (New York, 1973).

International Accounting Standards Committee, *Treatment of Changing Prices in Financial Statements: A Summary of Proposals* (IASC, 1 March 1977).

The Institute of Chartered Accountants in England and Wales, *Survey of published accounts, 1976* (ICAEW, 1977).

Michael C. Jensen, 'The Foundations and Current State of Capital Market Theory', in Michael C. Jensen (editor), *Studies in the Theory of Capital Markets* (New York, 1972).

Ralph Coughenor Jones, *Effect of Price Level Changes on Business Income, Capital and Taxes* (American Accounting Association, 1956).

Michael Lafferty, *Accounting in Europe* (Cambridge, 1975).

Baruch Lev, *Financial Statement Analysis* (Englewood Cliffs, 1974).

Ronald M. Marshall, 'Determining an Optimal Accounting Information System for an Unidentified User', *Journal of Accounting Research* (Autumn 1972).

Russell Mathews and John McB, Grant, *Inflation and Company Finance* (Sydney, 1957; 2nd ed., 1962).

Richard Mattessich, *Accounting and Analytical Methods* (Homewood, 1964).

Maurice Moonitz, *Obtaining Agreement on Standards* (American Accounting Association, Studies in Accounting Research, No. 8, 1974).

K. Michael Oldham, *Accounting Systems and Practice in Europe* (London, 1975).

Price Waterhouse, *A Survey in 46 Countries: Accounting Principles and Reporting Practices* (Price Waterhouse International, 1975).

George H. Sorter, Selwyn W. Becker, T. Ross Archibald and William H. Beaver, 'Accounting and Financial Measures as Indicators of Corporate Personality', in Robert K. Jaedicke, Yuji Ijiri and Oswald Nielsen (editors): *Research in Acccounting Measurement* (American Accounting Association, Collected Papers, 1966).

Edward Stamp, 'ED18 and Current Cost Accounting: A Review Article', *Accounting and Business Research* (Spring 1977).

Peter E. M. Standish, 'Can Financial Reporting Survive Morpeth?' *Accountancy* (July 1977).

Peter E. M. Standish, 'Proposals for Reform of Australian Company Financial Disclosure Requirements', in *Australian Company Financial Reporting* (Australian Society of Accountants, Bulletin No. 18, May 1975).

Peter E. M. Standish, *The Theory of Corporate Financial Reporting* (The Australian National University, Department of Accounting and Public Finance Monograph No. 3, 1975).

George J. Staubus, *A Theory of Accounting to Investors* (Lawrence and Berkeley, 1961).

Robert R. Sterling, *Theory of the Measurement of Enterprise Income* (Lawrence, Kansas, 1970).

Arthur L. Thomas, *The Allocation Problem: Part Two* (American Accounting Association, Studies in Accounting Research No. 9, 1974).

Stephen A. Zeff, *Forging Accounting Principles in Five Countries* (Illinois, 1971, Arthur Andersen & Co. Lecture Series).

An Investor's View

by

DAVID H. LeROY-LEWIS

CONSIDERATION of the general theme of this conference has been a somewhat daunting task, but a salutary one, and leads one readily to appreciate that a conference devoted to the present state of financial reporting and of accounting standards is very appropriate at this time. This address will seek to make some assessment of the view which investors take of the profession's progress towards a comprehensive definition of accounting standards; but in addition attention will be drawn to certain similarities in the present position of the accountancy profession and the securities markets.

The Investor

Until 1950 most of the shares and other securities issued by British Companies were owned by private individuals. In 1957 they owned 66 per cent of the Ordinary Shares of Companies listed by the Stock Exchange. By 1970 this figure had fallen to 47 per cent. Over the same period the proportion owned by institutions (insurance companies, pension funds, investment trusts and unit trusts) rose from 17.9 per cent to 31.7 per cent. Since then the personal sector has disposed of company securities worth about £8,000m. which could represent approximately a further 15 per cent of the total. There are a variety of reasons for this movement but it reflects in the main the tax advantages of saving through life assurance policies and pension funds together with demands on individuals made by high — nowadays penal — taxation, by inflation and by falling living standards. This large increase in the proportion held by institutional shareholders must be recognised and taken into account in arriving at the 'investor's view', since the skilled investment manager cannot be expected to have quite the same view as the ordinary individual investor.

Because of this shift in the type of shareholders, the market has tended to become dominated by the institutional investors with professional investment managers and departments. The investor's view has as a result become very professional requiring sophisticated standards of reporting by companies.

The Stock Exchange

The principle functions of the Stock Exchange are firstly to provide a trading market, known as the secondary market — which offers (insofar as this can ever be achieved) the best possible opportunity for honest and equitable trading whether it be in new issues, ordinary trading transactions, mergers and takeovers. Secondly, it seeks to provide the mechanism for the raising of capital by means of the issue of securities i.e. the new issue or primary market. The over-riding principle, so far as investors are concerned, is the provision of equality of information and of opportunity between shareholders large and small, those close to the Stock Exchange and those far from it.

Part of the function of the Stock Exchange itself, as distinct from the members, is to regulate the market, a role which will be briefly described later. In this regulatory function it is assisted in limited and specialist roles by the Institutes of the Accountancy Bodies and since 1968 by the Panel on Takeovers and Mergers. The Stock Exchange's role falls into two parts, the internal surveillance of members' activities and the external regulation of the listed companies.

Control over the actions of stockbrokers and jobbers is exercised by the Council of the Stock Exchange by virtue of the rules and regulations of the Stock Exchange. These are similar to those under which the Institutes within the profession act, although they are probably more extensive.

The external regulation of the listed companies is exercised by the Stock Exchange through the Listing Agreement which is accepted voluntarily but formally by the boards of all listed companies through the adoption of a standardised board resolution. It imposes on the company obligations to maintain certain future standards.

It should be appreciated that in the United Kingdom there is no statute which sets up the Stock Exchange or endows it with any authority. The very great authority and influence, which the Council of the Stock Exchange in the United Kingdom does enjoy, is voluntarily assumed, having been built up over a great many years. That authority is voluntarily acceded to by those who use the market.

This self-regulation seeks to provide a system of controls which enables appropriate ethical standards to be laid down and enforced. When actual fraud is discovered it is properly dealt with by the authorities under the law. Self-regulatory controls are not concerned with crime or civil wrongs. They seek to establish, and exist to enforce, ethical standards on Members of the Stock Exchange, bankers and other professional advisers, on company directors, shareholders and investors generally that go far beyond the requirements of the criminal or even civil law. Departures from these standards of good behaviour, which are intended to protect investors from unfair treatment, are regarded as constituting misconduct on the part of those concerned. The appropriate sanctions for such misconduct are imposed by the relevant authority whether that be the Council of the Stock Exchange or some other body. The rules and disciplines under which such sanctions are operated are drawn up in commonsense terms and are flexibly interpreted. In practice self-regulation is believed to give greater protection to investors than could be achieved by the relatively ponderous and complex machinery of law. Self-regulation has the supreme advantage that under the law marginal conduct is either criminal or permissive — under self-regulation marginal misconduct is still misconduct. Self-regulation seeks to enforce what is fair. The law can only be concerned with what is lawful.

It would at this point, however, be foolish to pretend that the whole concept has not been given a thorough going over lately. It is not only the authority of the Stock Exchange which has been called in question. The debate, which was initiated in 1974 by the Department of Trade enquiring into the arrangements for the supervision of the securities markets, has been accompanied by strident voices criticising the effectiveness of the supervision exercised by the ruling bodies of the accountancy profession. Auditing failures have been given much publicity, and the profession has responded sensibly, if perhaps somewhat tardily, by asking Lord Cross to examine the disciplinary situation within the profession. At about the same time the Secretary of State for Trade, in a notable statement last October, expressed considerable faith in the concept of self-regulation; and while both the profession and the Stock Exchange are in due course going to have to satisfy the Wilson Committee, it is to be hoped that with some modifications — for no doubt improvements can be made — the present system will be allowed to remain intact.

The Present Position of the Stock Exchange

Since 1929 the growth of the capital market has been centred upon the Stock Exchange. In monitoring this growth the Stock Exchange has adopted a philosophy of disclosure rather than supervision. During this period it has enforced its requirements through the voluntary acceptance by the listed companies and their advisers that what it was doing was fair, was needed and was in general terms equitable as between the issuers of capital and the providers of that capital. The Stock Exchange requirements have at all times been in advance of the law and have often been enacted after a suitable period of trial. Some landmarks and innovations adopted by the Stock Exchange during this period are:

Development of prospectus requirements (Appendix 34) and other measures of investor protection in the 1930s.

Consolidated accounts requirements, 1946 (pre-Companies Act).

Recognition of the virtue of non-statutory rules in the 1948 Companies Act through the adoption of the Certificate of Exemption provisions.

Acceleration of disclosure in 1950s and 1960s.

So much for the history. At the present time the Stock Exchange is not and cannot afford to be complacent. A pause is taking place in the development of this story of disclosure and self-regulation — a pause which, though perhaps it is not fully realised, has been caused by a desire to stop and re-examine where this road of disclosure, and more disclosure, is leading.

Until 1974 the Stock Exchange led the way in the growth and increased sophistication in disclosure standards receiving general approval for its actions. During this period the position of the Stock Exchange was reinforced by the fact that, owing to the unified nature of the capital market, long term capital could only be obtained by coming to the market, submitting to the Stock Exchange's listing requirements and subscribing to the Listing Agreement. This position still exists but now, except for the rights issues in 1975 and 1976, the demand for capital has been much reduced due to the present political and economic conditions.

The year 1974 was the watershed of this stage of development and perhaps the significance of the unexpected and devastating market collapse has not yet been fully appreciated. Banking confidence suffered very severely and whole sectors, particularly the secondary banks and property companies, were close to total failure.

There was a substantial loss of confidence on the part of the private investor who saw his personal invested savings almost disappear within a desperately short space of time. There is no evidence yet that he has recovered from that traumatic experience and is prepared to venture back to the market. It is difficult to be sure whether failure yet to return to the market is still due to the events of 1974 or whether it is due to the factors mentioned earlier — high inflation rates, a pay freeze and penal taxation.

In addition, the companies sector has been affected in two distinct ways. Firstly, the market is still at a level at which directors of companies are still unable to sell their shares at prices which match even the book value, let alone the replacement cost, of their assets. In those circumstances companies simply are not prepared to come to the market for the directors believe that, at current market levels, they would be giving their companies away. Secondly, and perhaps not so well appreciated is the belief on the part of a number of companies that they suffered unduly in the market collapse in 1974 simply because their shares were listed on the Stock Exchange. Some of them were subject to almost daily examination by financial commentators and almost certainly in some cases — in for example the building industry and the property industry — creditors, who might otherwise have been content to accept normal terms or even to accept some delay, were led to demand much swifter repayment than normal. These factors have tended to alter people's attitudes towards the benefits in general terms of being listed and have, together with the other market factors, drawn attention to what has suddenly appeared as the disadvantages which flow from the amount of disclosure involved in having a listing.

In addition, some controlling directors and/or shareholders are believed to be disgruntled with the way they think the market has treated them. Of course, if this is so, it indicates a certain misunderstanding of the role of the market. The price of a share in the market is not decided solely upon the value of the net assets of a company. It is a price based at any one moment upon supply and demand on a willing buyer, willing seller basis with the jobbing system equating these two forces. However irritated shareholders may be at the low price level of their shares in the market, it must be remembered that, providing there has been full disclosure, the price in the market is what investors believe to be fair, having regard to all the circumstances and conditions at the time.

There is too a reduction in the number of companies at present seeking a listing. This lack of demand for new capital may be the result of uncertainty in the market, of the effects of 'crowding out' by the Government having to raise money to meet the Public Sector Borrowing Requirement with the consequent high interest rates, etc. But the reluctance in submitting to the disclosure provisions is at least a contributory factor for this state of affairs.

So far as the Stock Exchange is concerned, it is not considered that there should be any withdrawal of the existing disclosure provisions. The Stock Exchange would, however, need to be thoroughly convinced of the need to adopt any new extension to the existing provisions. It is very conscious of the problem the S.E.C. in Washington are facing with the extent of their disclosure provisions both in the terms of reluctance of companies to comply, the lack of use made of the information disclosed, and the burden of expense imposed on the companies in preparing the information. It has been noted that recent legislation requiring the public disclosure within five days of share dealings by directors is in fact acting as a discouragement to directors from having personal or family shareholdings in their companies, and tends to encourage them to hold shares in their competitors. In that way they suffer no interference with their freedom to deal as they wish and yet they have personal knowledge of the relevant trading conditions. This is scarcely a desirable development from the investors' point of view.

The Stock Exchange is sometimes urged to have two types of listing, with differing standards of listing requirements. This idea suffers from the disadvantage that in the U.K. there would appear to be no incentive for a company to move from a lower list to the higher list, i.e. to full listing. To adopt two lists would appear to be counter-productive in terms of maintaining the existing high listing standards, although temporary concessions have been made in the case of the North Sea oil companies. It is doubtful whether this step would have any real relevance to the problem.

Finally, there is the question as to whether the Stock Exchange should establish a different market for trading in the shares of companies unable or unwilling to subscribe to the accepted listing requirements. This suggestion ignores the fact that there is an existing facility frequently used for dealing in the shares of unlisted companies but as a special deal with the prior consent of the Quotations Department and not on a continuous market basis. Perhaps more emphasis should be given to this facility.

The Stock Exchange has not, however, halted the development of the self-regulatory process during this pause. It is planning to issue within the next few months a code of conduct for directors' share dealings. The code, which will be a model of good practice, will be attached to the Stock Exchange Listing Agreement. We hope the code will be issued by mid-summer and will be helpful to those concerned.

Another area where a code of conduct might be worthwhile is in the field of public share issues, particularly with regard to issuing houses and reporting accountants.

Lastly, the Stock Exchange is working closely with the new Department of Trade/Bank of England joint review body on City institutions in order to improve the self-regulatory processes. This again must benefit the investor.

Requirements of Investors

When considering the requirements of investors so far as financial accounting is concerned, the existence and significance of a very extensive and capable financial press in the United Kingdom should not be overlooked. No country in the world has a financial press that is so widely read, so varied in its range of comment and so extensive in its coverage of company news. The financial press reports, analyses and generally acts as a watch dog over company affairs and in this role is a real benefit to the investor. As has previously been indicated, however, some of its activities are not happily accepted by the companies, particularly during periods of falling markets and acute economic uncertainties.

In broad terms investors require the following to be applied to financial reporting by companies:

Consistency This is just as essential in the accounts for shareholders as it is in management accounts.

Simplicity Here a compromise is needed. Financial reports must be sufficiently simple as to be comprehensible to individual shareholders and yet sufficiently detailed to enable the analysts of institutional investors to examine, probe and monitor in sufficient depth the financial results of the companies as well as to be able to form a judgement upon the management results.

Comparability The 'discipline of the Market', i.e. the interlocking relationship between one share and another, is one of the pillars of an efficient trading market, and requires the ability easily to compare one company with another, particularly those in the same section of industry or trade.

Accounting Standards

Accounting standards have had to be adopted by the accountancy profession in order to make it more certain that the financial reporting by companies complies with the aims of consistency and comparability. The need for these in modern society is so pre-eminent that guide-lines must be issued so as to influence, but not adversely impair, the exercise of the judgement of company boards. But above all accounting standards from the investor's point of view must re-affirm the economic realities governing commercial life, e.g. by adopting a 'system of value accounting' which must be consistent and which must continue to measure corporate performance, first and foremost, in commercial terms and in a way that facilitates comparability.

It may well be that 'social balance sheets' and other such things will follow but they should reflect the expressed need of investors and not be designed just to satisfy the curiosity of other groups. Above all, they must not be allowed to obscure the fundamental purpose of the company, which is to make profits for its proprietors. That is the only way the company will remain alive, will thrive and expand, and unless it does these things, it will not be able to raise more capital to create more jobs and to pay higher wages. It will not in fact be able to play its part in the creation of wealth on which the wellbeing of the nation and the success of the company so depend.

The Stock Exchange and the Accountancy Profession

Reference has been made to the way in which the Stock Exchange works both in its capacity as a trading market and in its regulatory role. It is in the regulatory role that the Stock Exchange and the accountancy profession have much to learn from each other.

The year 1969 was a critical point in the life not only of the securities industry but also of the Stock Exchange and the profession. Self-regulation was being quesioned on two accounts — the ethical propriety of City behaviour in takeover bids and the credibility of published accounts. These aspects came together in the cases of A.E.I. and Pergamon. I will not dwell on them — they have passed into history — the City came through that testing time mainly due to the birth of the Takeover Panel and the support given to it. The profession also responded by taking a great step forward in setting up the ASSC and it would be right here to acknowledge and pay tribute to the great part that Sir Ronald Leach played in this body until very recently. The profession and indeed the securities industry owes a great debt to Sir Ronald for his initiative and drive in his work as Chairman of this Committee. We must wish the next speaker well in his succession to this 'bed of nails'. It must be a somewhat forbidding prospect for Sir William particularly when his first two problems are Deferred Taxation and ED18. During this critical period in 1969 the problems for the securities industry and the profession were similar. For the securities industry the regulations were largely already written; the supreme test for the City was enforcement. For the profession, the problems of writing the rules were — and still are — uppermost in people's minds. But enforcement is now the question for the accountancy profession as well as the Stock Exchange and will remain a problem for the future.

This is not to say that the profession has ever failed to recognise the problem. The original concept for its solution was to invoke the loyalty owed by individual Chartered Accountants to their professional body. This concept has had some fair success so far as accountants in professional practice (as auditors) are concerned, but appears to have failed so far as accountants employed outside the profession are concerned. It is doubtful whether it was ever likely to succeed in that respect. Conflicts of loyalty involving one's profession on the one hand and one's employer on the other are situations which are best avoided.

The question of enforcement by the profession threw into clearer focus the part which the Stock Exchange could play via the Listing Agreement. This Listing Agreement imposes upon companies a standard of conduct which goes beyond that required by statute. The various areas where this specifically applies have not been detailed except to draw attention to one provision. Most significantly in the context of this address the Listing Agreement provides that the company's report and accounts should be prepared in accordance with the statements of standard accounting practice. This then is how the accounting standards are actually imposed upon listed companies whilst minimising any possible conflicts that might arise between those in the profession and those outside.

The Future of Accounting Standards

There is no doubt that the investor should support and be grateful to the profession for its progress towards defining accounting standards, since they support the requirements of the investor for consistency and comparability in financial reporting.

The quasi legislative procedures by which these accounting standards are defined, however, need to be kept under the most careful scrutiny. Flexibility must be the keynote of any approach to this aspect. The profession must always keep in mind that it legislates by consent, not only so far as its own members are concerned but also, and perhaps more importantly, so far as the companies are concerned.

The Stock Exchange, which has often experienced — indeed is now experiencing — similar problems in relation to the Listing requirements or even the Listing Agreement, believes that ideally an acceptable solution to such difficulties can only be arrived at by ensuring that the complainant does have the right — and knows he has the right — either directly or through a skilled agent to argue his particular case. It is not only the provision of such a safety valve, but the knowledge that such a safety valve does exist that is so important. Obviously such a procedure can rarely apply in the profession and so the back-up procedure becomes of even greater importance. Governing by consent requires the active understanding of the reasons for the various rules and regulations by those who are governed. Enforcement depends to a very great extent upon their voluntary acceptance of this quasi-legislation. The most likely way of obtaining this aceptance is by ensuring that what is being proposed is known and interested parties or their representatives should be actively encouraged one way or another to make their views known and to participate both in the formulation of the standard and in the dialogue after the draft legislation is published. In this connection a discussion document in the form of a Green Paper can be of great value as a precursor to an exposure draft. The profession, whilst quite properly acting as the leader in this field, should also act as an advocate both before the preparation and after the production of the exposure draft.

Much of this is realised and much is being done, but comments are heard from time to time that there actually is less access to the law makers in the context of accounting standards than if it were a matter of a Parliamentary Bill. This is a criticism which cannot be ignored when those, who believe in self-regulation, are propounding the advantages of proceeding otherwise than by way of statute. There is also another reason. It has been explained that the Stock Exchange through its Listing Agreement enforces the requirement that listed companies do comply with definitive accounting standards. When there is dissatisfaction over an accounting standard, even when it is only proposed and before it has become definitive, the Stock Exchange often receives comments or representations. If there is any dissatisfaction some of it does rub off on the Stock Exchange because of the compliance requirement in its Listing Agreement. The Stock Exchange therefore has a very real interest not only in the contents of accounting standards but also in the measure of their acceptance. Finally, the Stock Exchange's interest arises from the fact that it is responsible for the trading market and it is in that trading market that the consensus of the views of investors turns itself into 'The investor's view'. From time to time this view includes opinions on accounting standards. Hence the validity of the Stock Exchange's interest and concern.

In this context the following single example demonstrates how decisions by the profession can affect the Stock Exchange. Any non-compliance with a definitive accounting standard requires an auditor to make an appropriate reference in his audit report. This has come to be regarded — particularly outside the profession — as a qualified audit report. The Stock Exchange itself would not normally regard a report containing any significant qualification or reservation as acceptable to support an application for listing. In the case of a qualified report appearing in an acquisition circular, the

Stock Exchange reserves the right to require that the approval of shareholders in general meeting be sought for the relevant acquisition. The S.E.C. in Washington is understood to have adopted a similar approach. Most people would regard it as counter-productive for there to be any increase in the numbers of qualified audit reports and it is for consideration whether it would be sufficient for the directors to issue the statement, as required under the Stock Exchange's Listing Agreement, specifying the reasons for adopting an alternative basis of accounting. In such a case the auditors would only have to make an appropriate reference in their audit report if the directors did not make a suitable statement. It would appear that this is an area which should be re-examined by the profession with other interested parties.

I.A.S.C.

It would be wrong to conclude this address without some brief reference to the work of the I.A.S.C., about which Sir William Slimmings will no doubt speak in greater detail. With the growing internationalisation of the securities industry, the investor must welcome the trend towards some standardisation in international accounts through the adoption of accounting standards. The difficulties are quite apparent; the rewards equally obvious. The Stock Exchange immediately backed the I.A.S.C. by indicating in the notes to the Listing Agreement that it supported the policy of the I.A.S.C. in formulating and publishing international accounting standards, It indicated its expectation that the accounts of listed companies, whether incorporated within the United Kingdom or elsewhere, should be prepared in conformity with the international accounting standards published by the I.A.S.C., any significant departure or non compliance being disclosed and explained. It is an ambitious, far reaching project which deserves the good wishes of all of us.

Conclusion

The shift of investor from individuals to institutions, encouraged presumably deliberately by Government taxation incentives, has resulted in investor requirements for more sophisticated standards of reporting by companies. The Stock Exchange and the profession have responded through enhanced listing requirements and the development of accounting standards. Both of these are enforced on listed companies by the Stock Exchange through the performance of its self-regulatory role. The profession also relies upon self-regulation in seeking to achieve acceptance of accounting standards by their members and the companies. The self-regulatory process avoids the disadvantage of inflexibility of a detailed statutory system and the ponderous and complex machinery of law. The near financial collapse in 1974 has caused a critical re-examination of the advantages of listing, although no fundamental criticisms appear to have emerged. Certainly the interests of investors would seem to require the retention and enhancement of the self-regulatory system. In this the Stock Exchange and the profession have a mutual interest. They must continue to work closely together because united they have a good chance of standing, divided they are certain to have to absorb the disadvantages of interference from outside. This would appear to be in nobody's interests, least of all the investors.

The Rôle and Responsibility of the Accountancy Profession

by

WILLIAM M. K. SLIMMINGS

IN OCTOBER 1970, I took part in a conference like this one, the subject being accounting and auditing in the 1970s. I began by saying it was a reasonably safe bet that throughout the decade a dominant subject of debate would be accounting standards and their repercussions on the auditor. In describing it as a *reasonably* safe bet, I was showing an inclination towards the kind of characteristically reckless speculation which would tempt me to back Oxford each way in the Boat Race.

The portents were all there. They had been taking shape over a number of years but they became more clearly visible in the late 1960s when take-over battles were much publicised. In a number of cases, the subsequently reported results differed substantially from forecasts made during the course of the battle, and when these differences appeared to derive from the application of different accounting practices it was very natural and reasonable for people to ask how they could possibly be justified. From there it was a short step to ask how the same firm of auditors could give an unqualified report on each of two sets of accounts which reflected the application of different accounting practices, and which thereby produced quite different results. The accountancy profession was under heavy attack.

It was Sydney Smith who once expressed surprise at hearing someone speak disrespectfully of the Equator. Shock rather than mere surprise was the profession's reaction to being spoken about so disrespectfully. We were not accustomed to such criticism. In the eyes of the public, we had been for many years the backroom boys; the chaps who did the sums, and, of course, got them right, because a sum can have only one right answer, can't it? *Quaere verum* was merely a question of *recte numerare*.

So far as news value was concerned, we had been a total loss. If a chartered accountant appeared in the papers at all, it was more likely to be in connection with some departure from his pin-striped respectability than with the work of the profession. This comfortable anonymity was probably not unwelcome to us, reared on reticence as we are, but it was not exactly complimentary as a public assessment of our importance, or unimportance, in the scheme of things.

Then, quite suddenly, everything changed. We had become news. Fleet

Street had turned the spotlight on us, and many of us had difficulty in adjusting our eyes to the glare. It was a highly uncomfortable transition.

When one is violently and unexpectedly criticised, there is a danger that one will over-react, in one or other of two extreme ways—either by taking up an excessively defensive posture, or by accepting the criticism too meekly with the risk of applying part of another Sydney Smith prescription—'Take short views, and hope for the best . . .' The very fact that the criticism is unexpected probably means that one is ill-prepared to answer it quickly and effectively.

In these circumstances, it seems to me all the more necessary that one should begin by seeing from whom the criticism comes, and by making as objective an assessment of its validity as one can. Such an assessment is necessary, both to determine what the response to the criticism should be, and to seek to ensure that the response is not only theoretically sound but also practically effective.

An analytical approach on these lines to the situation as it existed at the end of the 1960s suggests first that the criticism did not come from the organisations that we as a profession serve *directly*. Indeed, these organisations—or, more specifically, members of the profession within these organisations—were themselves the target for criticism. It is perhaps not too broad a generalisation to say that non-practising members of the profession were criticised for the quality of the financial reports published by their organisations, and that the practising members were criticised for not doing a satisfactory job in reporting, in their role as auditors, on the 'truth and fairness' of these financial reports.

From whom, then, *did* the criticism come? To some extent, from Government, or agencies of Government; to some extent, from regulating agencies like the Stock Exchange; to some extent, ironically enough, from the profession itself, via post-mortem reports on situations where investigations had been found necessary; and, very naturally, the Press and other media were there either as reporters of what these critics were saying, or as spokesmen themselves for an amorphous body of 'users' of financial reports. The wave of 'consumerism' was beginning to roll, and although it opens up a much wider subject than is pertinent to this paper, it is perhaps worth remarking that the accountancy profession was far from being the only one in danger of being engulfed: there was evidence of a more general unwillingness to give automatic credence to the hitherto unquestioned experts.

At the conference in 1970 which I mentioned at the beginning of this paper, I tried to make a dispassionate analysis of the criticisms levelled at the profession, and I suggested that there were three main grounds on which we could legitimately be criticised:

(1) We had not succeeded in getting across to the unprofessional reader that the figures in the annual accounts of a continuing business must

represent to a greater or lesser extent matters of judgement rather than of specific measurement. This was the basic irony, that we had been credited with a degree of certitude, almost of infallibility, which we had never thought of claiming for ourselves.

(2) We had failed to give any clear indication in accounts as to the bases on which they had been prepared.

(3) We had allowed too great a proliferation of 'acceptable' accounting practices, and had not merely sanctioned but had approved differences of accounting treatment where circumstances did not justify these differences.

To some extent the three grounds overlap, but broadly it may be said that the first two represent clear failures of communication, while the third goes to the root of the matter of the formulation of accounting standards. There were, and are, those who argue strongly that the first and third grounds cannot be wholly consistent, *inter se,* because anything approaching a rigid uniformity in the presentation of accounting information is incompatible with the variety of circumstances which the information is designed to represent. Mr. Arthur Morison, for example, put the case for flexibility this way, in a paper which he gave to the Summer School of the Institute of Chartered Accountants of Scotland in the summer of 1970:[1]

> ... Accounts present a picture of economic facts ... There are at present a great many permissible accounting conventions which the accountant can choose from; nothing in the logic of the discipline itself prescribes which one he shall choose. And the area of the permissible is itself continually changing. The object is simply to present a picture of the facts; the means are a set of conventions using both figures and (may we not forget) words. The restraints on what is said are therefore empirical and subjective, not logical or demonstrative. Firstly, what are the facts? Secondly, what picture will most fairly present them? The concern is wholly with the truth ...
>
> The object of the balance sheet is to present an estimate of where the business now is, and the object of the profit and loss account is to present an estimate of how it is doing. An estimate is something which *ex hypothesi* one does not exactly know; there may be many careful estimates (many pictures) of one fact, and they may all be wrong. This does not prove that the people who made them were felons; it suggests that some facts are difficult to know and to describe. 'Where a business now is' and 'how a business is doing' are things which are very difficult to define, know or describe. They depend as much on the future as on the past: this is the key difficulty. One is seeking to convey a picture of things that (in any complex case) cannot possibly be fully known until long after they have ceased to matter. The hall-mark of accounting, as of all commercial activity, is uncertainty ...

The power of free and rational argument remains the best road to the truth in human affairs. I would therefore give companies the maximum freedom to present their accounts in whatever way they thought fit, and would then require them to *explain* and *justify* the course they had taken.

The auditor's task — no light one! — would be to ensure that they did. And to see that they did it fairly.

Despite the attractiveness of Mr. Morison's argument particularly perhaps to members of an Institute whose motto is *quaere verum* and who have always had a high regard for a sturdy independence of thought, I guess that there were a great many members of the profession who had become uneasy about the 'great many permissible accounting conventions which the accountant [could] choose from', and who had come to think that the great many were too many. That was certainly the view which was implicit in the action of Sir Ronald Leach, then President of the English Institute, when he took the initiative in the setting up of the Accounting Standards Steering Committee at the end of 1969, an initiative which was supported by the other principal accountancy bodies in the United Kingdom. For many years, of course, the English Institute had issued recommendations on accounting principles, but being recommendations these were advisory rather than mandatory. The setting up of the Accounting Standards Steering Committee implied an admission that something more stringent was needed.

So far, I have been talking in a United Kingdom context, but the situation as I have tried to describe it was not peculiar to this country. Much the same kind of thing was happening in other countries throughout the world, and the profession in these countries was therefore facing the same kind of problems as we were.

I have suggested that the general shape of these problems was becoming evident at the beginning of this decade. Developments during the last seven years have defined their shape more clearly, but in some respects still sharper definition is needed. I would summarise what is already evident and what is not yet fully evident as follows:

(1) It is evident that financial reporting and accounting standards must be looked at as parts of one problem: what is not yet evident is how the solutions of the parts will be fitted coherently together.

(2) It is evident that the accountancy profession will be held accountable for finding solutions, and that this is a responsibliity we must accept. We have to accept, as a general proposition, that our audience in future is going to be a much wider, more enquiring, more demanding and more critical audience than we have been accustomed to, and that we must direct ourselves to meeting the legitimate needs of that audience. What is not yet evident is just who will comprise that audience, and what their legitimate needs are. In accepting responsibility for accountability, we are entitled to ask 'accountable for what,

to whom?' We must not allow legitimate needs to expand into expectations that would be impossible for us to meet, or that would make quite unreasonable demands upon us. And we need to find a proper reconciliation between the interests of those whom we serve directly, and those in the wider audience, however defined, who are users of the information contained in financial reports.

(3) It is evident that Government intervention, irrespective of the political complexion of the Government, is likely to grow in matters which we have hitherto regarded as our preserve. What is not evident yet is where the line will be drawn between regulation by the profession and regulation by statute, but it seems likely that this will depend upon the extent of our success in meeting the challenges we are facing.

(4) It is evident that problems of financial reporting and accounting standards have to be faced on an international as well as on a national basis. The greater sophistication of the capital market and the growth of international operations accompanied by the breaking down of national boundaries through organisations like the European Economic Community point clearly in this direction. What is not yet fully evident is how the necessary harmonisation of financial reporting and accounting standards on an international scale will be achieved.

(5) It is evident that acceptance of the need for a body of accounting standards will carry with it acceptance of the need for a monitoring procedure to see that the standards are observed. It is not yet fully evident what the nature of that procedure will be, nor what the sanctions will be in the event of failure to comply with the standards.

Work in identifying the users of financial reports, and the legitimate needs of these users, is proceeding in a number of countries. The Canadian Institute, for example, has set up a four man group to study the objectives of corporate reporting, and they expect to report later this year. In the United States, the Financial Accounting Standards Board has set in motion a similar enquiry,[2] but some evidence of the way that the collective mind of that country's Securities and Exchange Commission is working may be gleaned from a talk given at the University of Missouri by Mr. John C. Burton, then Chief Accountant of the Commission, on 'The changing face of financial reporting'.[3] The tone of Mr. Burton's talk was set by his opening sentences:

> In a rapidly changing world such as we have today the standard by which financial reporting must be judged cannot imply static goals; rather, it must serve as a constantly moving target which must be pursued.

Mr. Burton stated the basic standard as follows:

> Financial reporting must reliably communicate the results of business activities to various interested parties on a timely basis.

He then went on to develop his ideas as to who the various interested parties are, and what a timely basis is, and he reached this conclusion:

> It seems inevitable that there will be a move toward a continuous reporting framework for public financial reporting. Management must think of its public reporting responsibilities throughout the year and not simply when annual or quarterly statements are due.

And he concluded by saying:

> A careful analysis of the demands of society suggests that a substantially changing face of financial reporting will be one of the realities that all who are involved in the process must recognise.

In the United Kingdom, the ideas implicit in Mr. Burton's talk have become more explicit. The Accounting Standards Steering Committee set up a working party to consider the subject of corporate reporting, and that working party has produced a discussion paper[4] which has provoked plenty of comment and criticism. Setting out to answer the question, 'Who should report what to whom', the working party has made proposals that many people find startling in their implications. It comes out with the view that 'there is an implicit responsibility to report publicly (whether or not required by law or regulation) incumbent on every economic entity whose size or format renders it significant'. It identifies seven user groups as 'having a reasonable right to information, and whose information needs should be recognised by corporate reports'. And it proposes that the information contained in those reports should extend well beyond the frontiers of conventional reporting. More specifically, it proposes that the following additional statements be published:

(i) A statement of value added
(ii) An employment report giving, *inter alia*, numbers employed, their location and age distribution, hours worked, employee costs, pension arrangements, education, trade union recognition and ratios stating sales, value added, profit, investment and remuneration on a 'per employee' basis
(iii) A statement of money exchanges with government
(iv) A statement of transactions in foreign currency
(v) A statement of future prospects
(vi) A statement of corporate objectives

The discussion paper also suggested that research be set in hand to examine the feasibility of multi-columnar reporting.

Not surprisingly, as I have said, these proposals have attracted a good deal of criticism, but it is significant that some of the working party's ideas were picked up in a consultative paper issued by the Government as a preliminary to consideration of changes in company law.[5] The formal reaction of the Accounting Standards Committee has been to say that it will initiate research work on each of the six additional statements proposed by the working party: it emphasises, however, that this does not imply that a standard will necessarily be issued, but only that the topic will be examined to determine whether it is an appropriate subject for a standard. It also recognises that other professions and disciplines must be involved in the implementation of any proposals that may emerge. This, I think, is most important. Although I believe that in the reporting of financial information the accountancy profession must play a leading role, we must not arrogate to ourselves the sole right to say what that information should be. It is not we who dictate the needs of users, and we have an obligation to make more rigorous attempts to identify these needs, and not merely to speculate about them. Do we, for example, have enough knowledge of the degree of sophistication of some of the most significant users of accounting information?

At the same time, we cannot accept the users' own definition of need uncritically. This is what I had in mind when I said that legitimate needs should not be allowed to expand into unreasonable expectations. We have to develop what is technically possible to meet users' requirements, but we have also to explain the practical constraints which limit the provision of information that would be highly desirable: forecasts are an obvious case in point.

The need for consultation arises also in the formulation of accounting standards, and this is a convenient point at which to say something about the Accounting Standards Committee, and how it works. I have already touched upon the circumstances which gave rise to its formation, on the initiative of Sir Ronald Leach, in 1969. At that time, although the other accountancy bodies were associated with it, it was a committee of the English Institute, and so it remained until its constitution was amended with effect from 1 February 1976. Its governing bodies are now the six principal accountancy bodies in the United Kingdom and Ireland (i.e. the three national Institutes of Chartered Accountants, the Association of Certified Accountants the Institute of Cost and Management Accountants and the Chartered Institute of Public Finance and Accountancy).

The Committee's objects are to propose for the approval of the Councils of the governing bodies definitive standards of financial accounting and reporting. These objects encompass

(i) fundamentals of financial accounting;
(ii) definition of terms used;
(iii) application of fundamentals to specific classes of business and
(iv) the form and content of financial statements, including presentation and disclosure.

The first point to note in these objects is that the ASC is not itself the standard-making body. Its job is to *propose* standards for the approval of the councils of the governing bodies: it is the Councils who have the ultimate responsibility for promulgating standards, and effectively a standard has to be approved by the Councils of each of the six bodies before it can be promulgated.

The normal drill in the production of a standard starts with a technical sub-committee being charged with the job of producing background papers on the subject under review. These papers will indicate the kind of matters which a standard will have to cover, and they may include the outline of a possible exposure draft. It is at this stage that the ASC normally gets down to debating the subject, and the debates can be prolonged. Ultimately, however, a proposed exposure draft should emerge, and at that stage the committee holds a ballot to ascertain whether a sufficient majority favours publication of the draft. The committee has a membership not exceeding 23, and the approval of a two-thirds majority of the *whole* membership (not merely of those voting) is required for the release of an exposure draft. Given the requisite majority, the committee is empowered itself to issue the exposure draft without reference to the councils of the governing bodies, but the draft has to make clear that it does not carry the authority of the councils.

An appropriate period of months is allowed for comment on the exposure draft, and at the end of the exposure period the comments received are collated and considered by the committee. In the light of the committee's assessment of these comments, the draft is amended, and at this stage the committee has to vote on it again, the question this time being whether it is suitable for transmission to the Councils as a proposed standard. As before, a two-thirds majority of the whole membership of the committee is needed before submission to the Councils can be made. Given the requisite majority, the proposed standard then goes to the Councils, and it is for them to decide whether to approve it, or not.

In the course of its work, the ASC has the advantage of periodical meetings with a consultative group representative of a wide spectrum of the business community and Government departments. These meetings provide the opportunity for discussion of what the committee is doing and what it hopes to do. I would like to see this kind of consultation extended to embrace discussions with sectors which can be identified as having a particular interest in the subject of a proposed standard, because the committee fully realises that if the standards which it proposes are to be effective they must command a wide measure of acceptability. We have to recognise, however, that although consultation is highly desirable, there are practical limits to the extent that it can be carried out.

You may find it surprising that so far the word 'inflation' has not appeared at all in my paper, nor have I mentioned the most notable, or notorious, of all exposure drafts, namely ED18 which sets out proposals for a system of current cost accounting. It is so wide-ranging a subject that it could monopolise several papers, and I must confine myself to making a few, possibly provocative, statements about it. (If they are provocative, they may provide matters for debate in the plenary discussions later on.)

(1) There is a very substantial body of opinion which says that, in the circumstances certainly of the last few years, accounts prepared in accordance with the historical cost convention do not give a true and fair view.

(2) If that opinion is accepted, the accountancy profession (not *ex cathedra*, but after proper consultation) has a duty to propose a method of accounting which provides a truer and fairer view than does the historical cost convention.

(3) This is what ED18 sets out to do. The mechanics of its preparation were more elaborate, and the extent of preliminary consultation far wider, than those I have sketched as normal practice in the preparation of an exposure draft.

(4) Some of the criticisms suggesting the need for a radical simplification of the proposals in ED18 raise a doubt as to whether there has been a full enough appreciation of the change of approach to accounting which acceptance of the proposals would require. Current cost accounting does represent a change from a historically-oriented approach to a value approach in the presentation of financial information, and that change is not going to be achieved if all that is done is, for example, to make an *ad hoc* adjustment to the charge for depreciation after the historical accounts have been prepared. Having said that, I would remind you that there is still a month to go until the end of the exposure period, and thereafter the massive job of collating and evaluating the comments on ED18 will take place. I hope that it will be possible to introduce some simplification without losing the essence of the proposals. What must not happen, I suggest, is that the accountancy profession should throw up its collective hands and say that it is all too difficult.

Now, and again it must be briefly, I would say something about international accounting standards. Although many countries had been working on domestic standards, there had been little in the way of international consultation; the result, not surprisingly, was a certain lack of coherence between the pronouncements that different countries issued on the same subject. Against the background of developments in the late 1960s which I have already sketched, the time was ripe for a move towards a greater measure of coherence by the time that the Tenth International Congress of Accountants was held in Sydney, in the autumn of 1972. The mood of that Congress clearly favoured the development of international standards, and only nine months later the International Accounting Standards Committee was born.

The United Kingdom representatives on the IASC are Mr. A. I. Mackenzie and Mr. J. P. Grenside. Past Presidents of the Scottish and English Institutes respectively. In the four years since it was set up, the IASC has got through a remarkable amount of work, but even that short experience has shown that the job of developing international standards is far from easy. Some of the more obvious problems are:

(1) How to promulgate effective standards on a truly international basis when commercial, industrial and professional practices in the constituent countries are in widely different stages of development. In other words, how to achieve a proper harmony between national and international standards. So far as the United Kingdom is concerned, work designed to achieve that harmonisation has reached an advanced stage. and I hope that the results of it will shortly be published. I think it is quite clear that we must aim to have only one 'book of rules' to which reference need be made in ensuring that accounts comply with all relevant standards.

(2) How to ensure that standards, once promulgated, are observed: what kind of teeth will be needed?

(3) How to ensure that an excess of zeal does not lead to over-regulation by way of standards. As a profession, we have always claimed as a supreme virtue the independence of thought of our members. How do we preserve a proper balance between the retention of that independence, and acceptance of the need for a body of standards?

The second and third of these points arise, of course, with similar force on domestic standards. A related point is the position of members of the profession in their role as auditors. In that role, I think that they must have a duty to monitor the observance of accounting standards, and to report non-observance, but how are they themselves to be monitored, as auditors? Can there be effective accounting standards without effective auditing standards? These are questions which I would enjoy hearing debated.

NOTES

1. *The Accountant's Magazine*, September 1970, Vol. LXXIV, No. 771, p. 410.
2. Financial Accounting Standards Board, *Conceptual Framework for Accounting and Reporting* (Stamford, 1974).
3. John C. Burton, 'The Changing Face of Financial Reporting', *The Journal of Accountancy* (February, 1976).
4. Accounting Standards Steering Committee, *The Corporate Report*, Discussion Paper (1975)
5. *Aims and Scope of Company Reports*, a preliminary draft paper prepared by the Department of Trade in May 1976 and circulated on an informal basis.

The Legal Aspects

by

R. B. JACK

IN THIS paper I shall try to examine the objectives of the law in imposing accounting obligations upon companies and in seeking to regulate how these obligations will be discharged. I have found it extremely difficult to elucidate a coherent philosophy underlying the development of the law in this respect. This is not entirely surprising. I have never forgotten a conversation I had with a very distinguished lawyer/civil servant now retired who had spent his whole working life in the Board of Trade and its successor ministries, preparing and supervising various legislative interventions into the field of company law. His view, no doubt motivated by a certain cynicism but nevertheless containing more than a grain of truth, was that you would look in vain at the statutory development of company law in the United Kingdom for any coherent philosophy because it represented to such a large extent a response to the latest scandal.

In parenthesis, I might comment that bodies such as the Stock Exchange, the Take-Over Panel and the professional accountancy bodies in the United Kingdom who have assumed the role of self-regulating agencies in this field are at least in danger of finding the pressures of public opinion as expressed through the media in particular situations so great that they will inhibit, if not preclude, the development of solutions within the self-regulatory system which are not mere reactions to particular points of difficulty but represent developments which can be justified in the whole context of what the self-regulation should be seeking to achieve. The accountancy bodies for example by their issue of Statements of Standard Accounting Practice could — and I have no doubt do — regard themselves as more than 'schools for avoiding scandals'. All I say, however, is that the legislative developments in this field will serve as perhaps a salutary warning to those who would seek to graft *ad hoc* solutions on to a fabric without due regard to its compatibility.

But while it is difficult to elucidate a coherent philosophy of the development of the law in this field it is perhaps not so difficult to identify the interests which have required the intervention of the law. I would seek therefore to identify these interests and then to make some attempt to assess how far the existing legal regulatory framework meets the present needs and how far it falls short of providing the measure of legal control which society expects in regard to financial statements.

The Protection of Creditors

The law's initial interest arose from the necessity to protect creditors of concerns which were given the benefit of limited liability. As Gower's *Modern Company Law*[1] succinctly puts it the [limited liability] company has only its capital to back its credit and, this being so, it is essential that capital should be more clearly defined and inviolable than is the case with an individual or partnership. The dictum of Lord Herschell in *Trevor* v. *Whitworth* is perhaps the classical exposition of the position. Lord Herschell put the position thus:

> The capital may no doubt be diminished by expenditure upon and reasonably incidental to all the objects specified. A part of it may be lost in carrying on the business operations authorised. Of all this persons trusting the company are aware and take the risk but they have a right to rely and were intended by the legislature to have a right to rely on the capital remaining undiminished by any expenditure outside these limits or by the return of any part of it to the shareholders.[2]

It is, of course, an essential corollary of the inviolability of capital that dividends must not be paid out of capital and that dividends must only be paid out of profits. Whether or not this rule has been observed by any particular company or its board of directors is essentially dependent on an accounting exercise. The series of legal decisions which there have been as to what constitutes distributable profit in a legal sense, serve only as guidelines to the application of accounting techniques. Furthermore these rules must now be considered as having been to a considerable extent overtaken by the concepts of what businessmen or accountants would reasonably regard as profits available for distribution. This has led to an increasing gap between what profits can be regarded as distributable in the legal sense as opposed to those which are regarded as distributable in the business sense. In many ways it is fair to say that the law has, as Professor Gower puts it, 'abdicated almost completely in favour of accountants and their businessmen clients in this area'.[3]

I am satisfied that the time has now come for the law to reassert itself in this area and that this reassertion should take the form of a definition embodied in statute of distributable profit which would accord with generally accepted practice. Even on the basis of historical cost accounting the absence of such a definition was a defect in the law and the introduction of CCA will emphasise this defect. The question of what constitutes distributable profit and the related question of dividends affects the rights of shareholders and of creditors and is not merely a question of accounting presentation. It is inexorably linked to the principle of the maintenance of capital which is central to the concept of limited liability as it is known in this country.

This is not the forum, and I am not the person to engage in a debate on the validity of the criticism of Exposure Draft No. 18 of the proposed statement of Standard Accounting Practice (ED18) by reason of its failure to define distributable profit. Nor do I regard it as being within the scope of this paper to indicate what elements would be essential in any definition of distributable profit. I have developed at least some of my thoughts in this area in another place. I hope I might however be forgiven if I repeat two comments which I made as I consider they have particular relevance to the subject of this particular paper.

The considerable measure of discretion, restricted only by a limited responsibility of disclosure, which ED18 has allowed to directors in deciding what figure to appropriate to revaluation reserve and in consequence what amount will be available for distribution by way of dividend would seem to strengthen the case for the more effective and relevant contraints on the exercise of these discretions which a statutory definition would provide. In the absence of any statutory guidance there seems to be a considerable prospect of conflict between industrialists and businessmen and their auditors who, faced with the discretions envisaged by ED18, may find it difficult or impossible to express a true and fair view opinion.

I also consider that in the course of the formulation of any definition of distributable profits there should be reconsideration of whether the principle of maintenance of capital as it has been up to now applied is sufficient protection to creditors dealing with a company the liability of whose shareholders is limited by law. I believe there is also a case for restating the principle in terms which would preclude the payment of dividends if the effect would be to reduce the value of the total assets below that of the capital 'after allowance has been made for the change in the value of money' during the period since its original subscription or at least from a date when the new definition becomes applicable, if that be later. (Here you will appreciate I am borrowing words from ED18 in regard to the Statement of the Shareholders Net Equity Interest.) Only in this way will the law restore to creditors the protection which it originally intended but which has been very substantially eroded as a result of the combined effect of the lawyers' abdication of responsibility, on the one hand, and the failure to devise accounting systems which clearly reflect the change in price levels on the other. The creditor and particularly the unsecured creditor has very much become the 'Tail-end Charlie'.

The Protection of Investors

Just as the need to ascertain profits in consequence of the legal concept of maintenance of capital has resulted in the development of accounting obligations so too has the fiduciary relationship imposed by law between directors and the company itself and its shareholders. This relationship arises from the fact while a company is a *persona* in law it is not in fact a natural person and can only act through directors or other agents exercising powers delegated to them by the company. As the Bullock Report on Industrial Democracy has been the latest to comment, there is a marked contrast between the fiduciary duties imposed upon directors and the relatively light duties of skill and care. The Report expressed the position thus:

> The common law duties of directors fall into two distinct parts; the fiduciary duties of loyalty and good faith and the duties of care and skill. The fiduciary duties require the director to act in what he believes to be the best interests of the company and to exercise his powers for the particular purposes for which they were conferred. He must not put himself in a position where his ability to do so is restricted or where there is a conflict between his duty and some personal interest. Of the many facets of this fiduciary duty the following seem to us of particular relevance. First, the director must not have outside interests which prevent compliance with his duty as a director of a company to act in its best interests, although so far this has not been applied to prohibit a director from being a member of a board of two competing companies. Second, the director must not make any secret profit (i.e. one not approved by the company) out of the execution of his office as director. Third, there is the problem of insider trading (i.e. a director making profits from dealing in shares or debentures on the basis of information known to him as a director). The Companies Act 1967 requires disclosure of a director's interests and those of his immediate family in his company's securities or the securities of its holding or any subsidiary company. Fourth, there is the question of confidential information. The exact ambit of the law of confidence is not clear; but there can be no doubt that in respect of companies' plans, projects, 'know-how', the director is under a duty not to reveal confidential information to outsiders.
>
> By contrast to these fiduciary duties the degree of care and skill to be shown by a director is not high and the Courts have had difficulty in deciding how much care and skill should be displayed by a director in carrying out his functions. A number of principles can be distinguished. A director is not obliged, in the absence of a contractual obligation, to give continuous attention to his company's affairs and he is, generally speaking, entitled to leave matters to properly delegated officers of the company so long as nothing 'puts him on enquiry' that something improper has been done. His liability for negligence is measured by a subjective duty of care, i.e. by the standard of what is reasonable for a person of his knowledge and his experience, although his conduct must not fall below what is considered

to be the reasonable behaviour of an ordinary man. There is scarcely any modern case in which a director has been held liable for mere negligence.[4]

This emphasis on the trusteeship or fiduciary character of the duties of directors has I think been reflected in the development of their accounting obligations. The Sandilands Report puts the position thus:

> It is a traditional tenet of accounting that the main objective of published financial statements is to enable the directors to give an account of their stewardship of the shareholders' funds to the shareholders.[5]

The Report specified two aspects of this type of accounting. The first was that the accounts should demonstrate to shareholders that their funds had been fully accounted for and that no illegal transactions had taken place; and the second was that accounts should provide information to shareholders to enable them to judge the efficiency of the management. It is an interesting speculation as to whether the law's preoccupation with the sanctity of trust obligations — a preoccupation the most recent manifestations of which are the emphasis on disclosure of directors' interests and the anticipated legal sanctions against insider dealing—may have been reflected in the development of financial reporting in respect of companies. In other words the first of the two aspects of accounting for stewardship as mentioned by Sandilands has enjoyed a measure of precedence over the second. Of course, any approach to accounting methods which places too great an emphasis on accountability as an aspect of trusteeship must be defective, ignoring as it does that the managers of a business concern (unlike the trustees of a purely trust fund, whose primary duty is the protection of the trust fund) must perforce take risks in pursuance of their primary duty to carry on a more or less speculative business in an attempt to earn profits for the company and its members. How long the law will be able to continue to take its somewhat relaxed view of the duties of care and skill which should be expected of directors must be a matter of speculation especially in view of the consideration which is currently being given to the role of the non-executive director. In view of recent experiences, the law would, I think, be out of touch with public opinion if it regarded non-executive directorship as 'little more than sinecures requiring at the most attendance at occasional board meetings'.[6]

It would, however, be wrong if we in fact threw the baby out with the bathwater and, in an attempt to produce financial statements which would act as some measure of the efficiency of management, and even as a guide to future performance, the fiduciary aspect was totally overlooked. It is, I think, still important for shareholders to know that their funds have been fully accounted for and that no illegal activities have taken place. The American debate about 'illegal and questionable payments' is perhaps a good illustration. Accounts do not really need to disclose whether or not bribes have been paid in Italy or the Lebanon in order to provide a guide to the performance of the management or the future profitability of the concern but a shareholder is entitled to know whether a company in which he has an interest does engage in such activities. There is no point in having an elaborate system of disclosure of directors' interests unless there is a means of having them conveyed to the shareholders through the report and accounts and subject to scrutiny by the auditors as their representatives. I accept the view expressed in the Sandilands Report[7] that the audit function is an essential part of any system of protection against improper use of funds. But I wonder whether the effective exercise of that function might be made more difficult if the emphasis on financial reporting was to move too far away from the concept of accounting for stewardship.

The *Ultra Vires* Doctrine

In this context perhaps a word about the *ultra vires* doctrine might not be out of place. This doctrine — as a result of the European Communities Act of 1972 — has been very substantially eroded in questions with third parties; and even before 1972 it was of limited application because of the wide powers taken by companies under their memoranda of association and the wide delegation of these powers to directors of the company. There remain, however, areas in which shareholders are entitled to be reassured by the auditors. If there are restrictions on the powers of the directors, for example in relation to borrowings, the shareholders should be told whether or not they have been observed. They should be advised also whether any payments or other arrangements have been made which cannot be regarded as being in the best interests of the company. This latter area is likely to become more complex if the recommendation of the Bullock Report is in fact implemented and the duties of directors are extended so that they are entitled to have regard not only to the interests of the shareholders but also of the employees of the company. Whether it will be possible to exercise any meaningful audit supervision on the directors' exercise of their powers if the interests which they have to consult are extended beyond the shareholders must be a matter of considerable doubt. The Corporate Report[8] issued by the Accounting Standards Steering Committee for comment and adopted by the Department of Trade as the basis of their discussion paper on the aims and scope of company reports[9] will raise very difficult questions for any persons involved in the audit function in relation to the accounts of companies.

The Philosophy of Disclosure

It has been repeated almost *ad nauseam* that the laws of the United Kingdom aimed at the protection of investors have very much pinned their faith on disclosure. The concept of full and frank disclosure first found expression in relation to prospectuses in what is known as the golden rule enunciated by Kindersley, V.C. in the following terms:

> Those who issue a prospectus holding out to the public the great advantages which will accrue to persons who will take shares in a proposed undertaking and inviting them to take shares on the faith of the representations therein stated are bound to state everything with strict and scrupulous accuracy and not only to abstain from stating as facts that which is not so but to omit no one fact within their knowledge the existence of which might in any degree affect the nature or quality of the privileges and advantages which the prospectus holds out as inducements to take shares.[10]

While this rule is stated in relation to prospectuses it has served as something of a guiding light in the development of the law in regard to the communication of information about the affairs of companies. The latest manifestation of the rule is to be found in the City Code[11] which effectively imposes on directors collectively and individually a 'golden rule' type obligation in regard to information communicated to shareholders in a take-over situation.

'A True and Fair View'

In ongoing situations, accounting obligations which the law has imposed for the protection of shareholders and potential shareholders are based on a dual obligation to give a true and fair view and to give the detailed information specified in the Companies Act. The Jenkins Committee[12] came to the conclusion that the general scheme of the Act in this respect was the right one in that it indicated in general terms the objectives and the standard of disclosure required and also prescribed certain specific information that must be given. The Report went on:

> The formula 'true and fair' seems to us satisfactory as an indication of the required standard while it makes for certainty to prescribe specific information which the law regards as the minimum necessary for the purpose of attaining that standard.

What is involved in the standard? Does 'true and fair' like 'fair and reasonable', 'just and equitable' and other similar expressions, mean what those who use them want them to mean? What constraints does the true and fair view concept impose in regard to the presentation of company accounts which would not be there if matters were left entirely to the detailed formulation of what must be disclosed with the ultimate protection lying in the general law against fraud and misrepresentation?

The Sandilands Report,[13] without quoting any authority, put forward the proposition that in general the Courts have accepted that the application of 'generally accepted principles' of accounting will lead to a true and fair view being shown. They did point out that the Acts gave only limited guidance to the accounting profession in interpreting the phrase 'a true and fair view' and that it had been traditionally left to the profession to develop accounting practices which are regarded as leading to a true and fair view being shown.

Can the law continue its abdication of responsibility in regard to the reliability of financial information? Or does the true and fair view concept need statutory amplification? And, as a related question, what standing should the law accord to the statements of standard accountancy practice issued by the accountancy bodies?

I suppose it is fair to say that the overriding requirement for accounts to provide a true and fair view has worked fairly well as measured against its objective of ensuring that accounts can reasonably be relied upon by investors and creditors of the concerns to which they relate. The words 'true and fair' taken together when applied to accounts seem, if experience is any guide, to impose on accounts the qualitative requirements of objectivity, realism, prudence, comparability and consistency which are among the qualitative requirements which the Sandilands Report[14] identified as being required of accounting systems.

There must, however, be doubts—and these doubts have clearly emerged in regard to the adoption of CCA — as to whether the concept of a 'true and fair view' is deficient in that on the one hand, it is too inflexible in the sense that it is tied to one particular system of accounting, namely, historical cost accounting, and on the other hand, that it is too flexible in that it does not impose any duty to select an appropriate frame of reference. The measure of recognition which has been accorded over the years to historical cost accounting must produce some degree of uncertainty as to whether accounts drawn up under any alternative system will be accepted as giving a true and fair view. In other words, can a change to a new accounting system be achieved and the accounts still give a true and fair view unless the new system has become a 'generally accepted accounting practice' in the sense of having standing by adoption over a long period of years?

Statements of Standards

The proposed introduction of CCA has brought to the forefront the question of the standing of statements of standard accounting practice. The debate centres round whether by the act of their promulgation they should acquire standing as formulations of generally accepted accounting practice, irrespective of whether or not they achieve the general support required to establish their appropriateness for adoption in accounts required to give a true and fair view. It is perhaps worthwhile reminding ourselves at this stage of the function that statements of standard accounting practice are intended to perform. The explanatory foreword to the statements[15] says that they are meant to provide descriptions of 'methods of accounting' approved by the bodies by which they were issued 'for application to all financial accounts intended to give a true and fair view of financial position and profit or loss'. Although it was envisaged that significant departures in financial accounts from applicable accounting standards should be disclosed and explained and the financial effects estimated and disclosed, it was not, however, the intention that accounting standards should provide a comprehensive code of rigid rules as it would be impracticable to establish a code sufficiently elaborate to cater for all business situations and circumstances and every exceptional or marginal case. Nor could any code or rules provide for innovations in business and financial practice. The explanatory foreword goes on:

> Moreover it must be recognised that there may be situations in which, for justifiable reasons, accounting standards are not strictly applicable because they are impracticable or, exceptionally, having regard to the circumstances, would be inappropriate or give a misleading view. In such cases, modified or alternative treatments must be adopted and, as noted, departure from standard disclosed and explained. In judging exceptional or borderline cases it will be important to have regard to the spirit of accounting standards as well as to their precise terms, and to bear in mind the overriding requirement to give a true and fair view.

Accounting standards were not intended to be inflexible but to be evolutionary. As the explanatory foreword puts it:

> Methods of financial accounting evolve and alter in response to changing business and economic needs. From time to time new accounting standards will be drawn at progressive levels, and established standards will be reviewed with the object of improvement in the light of new needs and developments.

In the light of the limited objectives and qualified application of the standards, what authority is it appropriate to attach to them in relation to 'the overriding requirement to give a true and fair view'?

At the risk of unnecessarily promoting my own views, I think the solution proposed by the Company Law Committee of the Law Society of Scotland, in which I was involved, was at least on the right lines when it argued for a statutory provision to the effect that, subject to the overriding requirement that accounts must give a true and fair view whatever method of accounting is utilised, the application of standard acounting practices from time to time current in Great Britain (and Ireland) will constitute *prima facie* evidence that the accounting methods used are a correct approach to the problem of determining a true and fair view.

The solution proposed seems to me to achieve a fair balance between the need to eliminate the possibility of an attack on accounts prepared on a new basis on the ground that they represent a departure from a 'generally accepted accounting principle' (be it historical cost accounting or any other system which may succeed it) and what the Sandilands Report described as 'the excessive and undesirable rigidity'[16] which would arise if accounting conventions were embodied in statute. It avoids too the effective delegation to the accountancy bodies of legislative competence to determine what constitutes a true and fair view which would be the consequence (clearly unacceptable from the point of view of public interest) of providing by statute that a standard promulgated by such bodies would be regarded as a generally accepted accounting practice.

But while the proposed introduction of CCA has perhaps pointed to the need to accord some higher authority to statements of standard accounting practice the problem created for companies in the interim period prior to the general adoption of CCA has highlighted the dangers of placing too great a reliance on 'generally accepted' accounting practice as meeting the true and fair view requirement. The difficulty arises thus.

If it is accepted that accounts which do not reflect the impact of changing price levels are incapable of giving a true and fair view — and that after all was the starting point of the whole exercise — it must be at least open to doubt whether a statement that accounts prepared in accordance with the historical cost convention give a true and fair view of a company's state of affairs and its profits, is not a contradiction in terms *unless the concept of a true and fair view involves only the application of an accounting system and does not concern itself with whether the system adopted gives the most realistic reflection of the true situation of the company*. That restricted interpretation of what is involved in a true and fair view is the only legal basis of the terms in which auditors are reporting during the interim period. If it is correct, then the true and fair view formulation seems to me to be falling far short of what I as a lawyer would have expected of it.

A Plea for Intelligibility

The Sandilands Report, in its exposition of the qualitative requirements of accounting systems, included among such requirements intelligibility. I am concerned that in an attempt to 'tighten up' the true and fair view concept it may be overlaid with so many detailed requirements, either in statutory form or in the form of practices recommended by the accountancy bodies, that accounts will cease to be intelligible to the layman and will only be comprehensible 'to a reader familiar with normal accounting practice and expecting it to be followed'.[17]

Mr. T. D. Lynch in his criticism of ED18 and current cost accounting generally put the matter quite clearly:

Annual financial accounts are prepared by accountants but they are not and should not be prepared for accountants. They should be prepared and presented with the consumer in mind albeit within the constraints and following strictly the rules and guidelines of accounting principles and of legal and other requirements.[18]

Or as Gower put it more colourfully:

As a result of the latest Companies Act it is generally agreed that published accounts are now mines of valuable information, supplying knowledge of the company's financial position in greater detail than is likely to be available from any other source. Clearly, the statutory provisions are not the last word on the subject; but in general they ensure that the vital information is there for those qualified to extract it. . . . The financial editor, the accountant and (sometimes) the lawyer can extract the gold from the mine, but the average investor lacks the technical skill. And the more detailed accounts become, the greater are his difficulties. In so far as he relies on competent professional advice no great harm is done, but all too often he has his flutter on the stock exchange or fills in his proxy form without taking this precaution. He may subsequently regret it — perhaps almost immediately if comment is excited in the financial Press (if he reads it) — but by then it may be too late. And what is true of the investor is even more true of the creditor. How many traders study published accounts before granting credit? And how many of them would draw the right conclusion if they did?

Published accounts have become the linch-pin of the system of protection through disclosure. Unless, in a Welfare State, this system is to be rejected in favour of some more drastic method, the outstanding need seems to be to ensure that accounts are presented in a form which is more readily intelligible to the layman.[19]

It seems to me a fair prospect that if anything like ED18 becomes generally adopted the gap between the layman and the expert will be widened with the result that a true and fair view will only be seen by those with special types of spectacles not available to the general public and certainly not under the National Health Service.

The Role of the Auditor

An essential feature in the present regulatory system is, of course, the requirement to have accounts reported on by auditors. The importance of the auditor's function has been recognised by the law by the powers which it has conferred on auditors and by its requirements on the standards of competence, the professional qualifications and the degree of independence which it requires of them. And to the law's requirements on independence the accounting bodies themselves have added weight in their attempt to ensure the total independence and absence of conflicting interests among auditors. It is true, of course, that they still owe their appointments in fact if not in law and look for payment to the directors on whose accounts they are called upon to report. The law, however, continues to rely at least by implication on the ethical standards of the profession and their rigorous pursuit of defaulters by their controlling bodies as the ultimate safeguard of the public interests in this area. These general statements in regard to the law's attitude to the auditor and his role are, I think, worthy of further development.

Last week, I found myself addressing a seminar of international lawyers on the subject of the responsibility of directors. The proximity in time of these two addresses, and the fact that I have not yet been able to impose on myself the self-discipline of getting down to the task of preparing talks until at least the eleventh if not the twelfth hour, caused me to regret very profoundly my impetuosity and unconscionable conceit in accepting both invitations. But in fact it was not all loss because it became clear in the course of the seminar that the development of the law of the United Kingdom and the extension of responsibility which the law and self-regulation is now imposing and will seek to impose on directors has a very close connection with their accounting obligations.

At the conclusion of my talk I suggested that non-executive directors were sitting in hotter seats than they had ever done, and I would say that that applies equally to auditors. What would be thought today of this judicial statement made at the end of last century of the duties of an auditor:

> An auditor, however, is not bound to do more than exercise reasonable care and skill in making enquiries and investigations. He is not an insurer. He does not guarantee that the books do correctly show the true position of the company's affairs. He does not even guarantee that his balance sheet is accurate according to the books of the company. He must be honest. That is, he must not certify that which he does not believe to be true and he must take reasonable care and skill before he believes that what he certifies is true. Where there is nothing to excite suspicion very little enquiry will be reasonably sufficient. Where suspicion is aroused more care is obviously necessary but still an auditor is not bound to exercise more than reasonable care and skill even in a case of suspicion and he is perfectly justified in acting on the opinion of an expert where special knowledge is required.[20]

The latest edition of Palmers' *Company Law* comments with some truth: 'While these general principles remain applicable the standards of reasonable care and skill are more exacting today than those which prevailed at the time when the above statement was made (in 1895).'[21]

What are the areas in which the law has raised its expectations of auditors?

In his role in relation to the proper application of the funds of the company the auditor's responsibilities, in so far as they arise from the *ultra vires* rule, have been made easier by the wide form in which the objects clause of memoranda of association are drawn and the wide delegation of powers to directors. It is, nevertheless, an important function. One has only to look at the highly sophisticated schemes which have been devised to get round the prohibition against loans to directors and the difficulty of avoiding a breach of Section 54 of the Companies Act 1948 (which prohibits the giving of financial assistance by companies in connection with the purchase of their own shares) to be aware of the continued difficulty of this aspect of the auditor's task. The investigation into the affairs of Slater Walker Limited is the most recent example of how near to the brink of the law entrepreneurs are prepared to go.

The auditor performs an essential function in relation to the observance of disclosure requirements. The disclosure philosophy which as I have said, is at the heart of the system of investor protection under the laws of the United Kingdom 'only works if the information disclosed can be safely taken as accurate. Unless checked by some independent outside authority this cannot be relied upon; so far as the accounts are concerned the auditors are this independent (and usually reliable) authority'.[22]

The Court's View

It is in relation to their functions of examining and reporting on the application of the company's funds and the correctness of the information disclosed that the judicial definitions of the functions of the auditor have been developed. The most famous is probably that the auditor 'is a watchdog, not a bloodhound'[23] and among the most recent is that of Lord Denning, which was couched in the following terms:

> An auditor is not to be confined to the mechanics of checking vouchers and making arithmetical computations. He is not to be written off as a professional 'adder-upper and subtractor'. His vital task is to take care to see that errors are not made, be they errors of computation, or errors of omission or commission, or downright untruths. To perform this task properly he must come to it with an inquiring mind — not suspicious of dishonesty, I agree — but suspecting that someone may have made a mistake somewhere and that a check must be made to ensure that there has been none.[24]

The Auditor as Arbiter

But the area in which, in my view, the duties of the auditor have been extended are in relation to his role as the ultimate arbiter of the true and fair view. It is perhaps going too far to describe this, as has one distinguished academic accountant, as a judicial function but there is at least a quasi-judicial element in it. The auditor must assess the accounts against some objective standard of what constitutes a fair and true view. Just as a judge decides what are the legal rules which are applicable and what result that produces in the case before him so the auditor on the basis of his knowledge and experience of what is generally accepted professional practice (including standards promulgated by accountancy bodies) decides whether or not accounts presented to him give a true and fair view. But if his consideration is judicial in character the method of arriving at it is not a judicial process. It is a decision arrived at on the basis of information supplied and sought. There must and should be a dialogue between the board and the auditors before the auditor gives his audit opinion and it is a dialogue which in a 'crunch' situation can easily develop into a confrontation, a contest of wills and of relative bargaining power.

For there are areas of debate between auditor and board which raise difficult and fundamental questions. For example, there must be clear room for difference of opinion in certain cases in regard to accounting policies involving as it does the selection of specific accounting bases which, to use the words of SSAP2, 'are appropriate to the circumstances (of the business enterprise) and best suited to present fairly its results and financial position'. In the recent liquidity crisis, which was no respecter of size or history in where it struck, auditors must have had many anxious moments as to whether they could accept accounts prepared on a going concern basis where there must have been serious doubts as to whether 'the enterprise in question would continue in operational existence in the foreseeable future'. (SSAP2's definition of the 'going concern' concept). But to incorporate these doubts in the audit report might well have put paid to any prospect of the enterprise's survival. This was clearly the dilemma which faced the auditors of British Leyland who have just reported on the accounts to 31 December 1976, in the following terms:

> These accounts have been prepared on the normal going concern basis which assumes that the company will continue to obtain finance as referred to in the paragraph headed 'Finance' set out in the Report of the Directors on page 14. (This is a reference to the provision of additional Government finance which was at the time of signing of the Auditors' Report by no means certain or unconditional.)
>
> On the basis set out in paragraph 2 above, in our opinion the accounts give a true and fair view of the state of affairs at 31 December 1976 and of the profit and source and application of funds for the period ended on that date, according to the historical cost convention, and comply with the Companies Act 1948 and 1967.

What does this mean? It is clear that if British Leyland is to continue it must get Government finance. But have the auditors in any way taken a view as to whether this finance will be forthcoming? I would think that the law might well expect auditors to have questioned the validity of such an assumption as the directors of British Leyland made in preparing their accounts on a going concern basis.

Requirement of disclosure of 'illegal and questionable payments', as in the United States, may be another area of dispute between a company and its auditors, especially when this may mean the end of a company's profitable operations in a particular country. In this area the doctrine of materiality may not necessarily be called in aid and a shareholder may legitimately require to know whether the company in which he has invested engages in 'questionable' business practices. That the amount is small in relation to the totality of the company's operations will not satisfy him.

One of the most common criticisms of ED18 is that it is too subjective so that CCA accounts will not be capable of audit. I take this to mean that it will be impossible to say whether they give a true and fair view. Professor J. C. Shaw, writing on 'The Implications for Auditors of ED18',[25] very properly pointed out that historical cost accounts have important areas of subjective judgement and all that ED18 would do would be to add new very significant areas of subjective judgement. He instanced deprival value (the value to the business of physical assets), deferred taxation (where a judgement has to be made of the likelihood of the liability emerging) and above all what part of the profit should be regarded as distributable and what 'should be retained within the business having regard to (the directors) assessment of its needs'. Under ED18 there will clearly be a much more extensive range of opinions which the auditor will require to validate before he gives his audit opinion. It is one thing for auditors to satisfy themselves about factual situations; it is quite another to pass judgement on the opinion of another. This is a sure way to lose friends and perhaps clients.

The law has to some extent recognised the difficulty and delicacy of the responsibilities it has imposed on the auditor. It has set standards of competence by prescribing the qualifications which are required. And I do not think that in this place and on this occasion I need to stress the educational obligation which that imposes on the recognised accountancy bodies. Professor Shaw put it thus:

> The accountancy profession will have to recognise the need for greater intellectual attainment than can be universally demonstrated just now from those who seek to practise as auditors. The auditors of the future will need more relevant and more demanding practical training and experience in order to inculcate and develop the personal attributes of intellectual integrity and moral independence.[26]

Although I accept the general thrust of Professor Shaw's remarks I am bound to speculate, somewhat mischievously I concede, on whether it will be possible to achieve the necessary levels of recruitment to the accounting profession if the entrants are to be measured against their capacity to achieve the high degrees of intellectual attainment, practical skill and experience and intellectual integrity and moral independence which Professor Shaw regards as necessary for those who seek to practise as auditors. There is in my experience no super-abundance of the gifts of intellect and character which will be required and whether those who possess them will be attracted to the accountancy profession must be at least open to doubt.

The law has also given a measure of statutory security of tenure of appointment to auditors. The Companies Act 1976 is the latest development in this area. But in practical terms it is difficult to continue when the board of directors want the auditor to go. The loss of a profitable audit is never a matter lightly to be countenanced. Access to shareholders at the annual general meeting when threatened with dismissal provides a limited measure of support to the embattled auditor. The qualification of his report which used to be thought a potent weapon in the hands of the auditors has now lost much of its effectiveness. Indeed it is not wholly a jest to say that any company worthy of its salt should expect and perhaps even demand to have its audit report qualified. We have come far from the time when a qualification was regarded as a 'red light'.[27]

The Auditor's Independence

By disqualifying persons connected with a company from acting as its auditors, the law has clearly marked its acceptance of the importance of the auditor's independence. The accountancy bodies, I know, have in mind the improvement of their ethical standards by moving to a situation where no auditor or any one associated with him can have any interest in the company audited. But the maintenance of independence is a difficult area. I sometimes think the failure to observe the law's demarcation between preparation and auditing of accounts is one of the most serious defects in our auditing system. It is perhaps unrealistic to expect, as the law does, that the two operations go on in isolation with those involved insulated from one another but, and this point was also made by Professor Shaw, the greater the involvement of the auditor in the preparatory work on accounts the more careful he must be to preserve his independence in auditing them. 'If the auditor is to continue to meet a socially necessary function he must jealously preserve his independence and integrity'.[28] That is clearly what the law expects of him!

An Audit Committee?

It has from time to time been suggested that the audit function will only be effectively performed when we have in the United Kingdom audit committees on the American model. It is argued that the audit committee is a more effective means of communication between board and auditors and will prevent too cosy and relaxed a relationship arising between the management of the company and its auditors. It will be an instrument of two-way communication, enabling the board to seek assurance from auditors as to scope of investigations and auditors to convey comments and criticisms of accounting systems and management which have emerged from audit. The committee could review matters of debate relative to the true and fair view assessment.

These are very worthy objectives but my doubts centre round the availability of the persons who will be required to serve on audit committees. Non-executive directors are the obvious candidates but can they do any effective job unless they have a sound working knowledge of accounting systems and practices. Otherwise, they will have to devote more time than can reasonably be expected of them to familiarise themselves with these techniques. And without persons with the necessary expertise to serve on them, audit committees will be quite incapable of realising the high expectations of those who advocate their introduction.

The alternative, of course, is for audit committees to consist of accountants but I doubt whether a professional closed shop will really produce the results which are claimed for audit committees. The process of preparation and auditing of accounts is perhaps too important to be left to the accountants.

The law then has given the auditor a status and armed him with powers which it considers necessary to enable him to carry out his functions. But it also imposes sanctions to secure that he does so competently and effectively or, to use the legal jargon, with reasonable skill and care. What this involves is clearly a developing concept with the development of accounting and auditing techniques. We have clearly moved on from the position taken by the court in 1896 when it found that the auditors were justified in relying on a certificate by the manager, 'a person of acknowledged competence and high reputation' as to the value of stock which subsequently turned out to be grossly overstated.[29] I have indicated earlier areas in which the courts may sooner rather than later seek to extend the responsibility of auditors beyond that which they have hitherto considered appropriate.

But if the extension of the auditor's legal liability in terms of the degree of skill and care he is expected to exercise may be a matter for speculation, there can be no doubt that the Hedley Byrne case[30] has already added a new dimension to the liability of auditors. This had previously been restricted to those to whom the auditors were in a contractual or fiduciary relationship. Although a strict view may not go as far as this, I would venture to suggest that the auditor's duty of skill and care is really now delictual in character in that it is owed to the whole world so that, if anyone can show that he suffered loss as a result of a mis-statement in the accounts and that such defect was attributable to a breach of the auditor's duty of skill and care, then the auditor will be liable. That is a prospect which should fairly concentrate the minds of auditors before they put pen to the paper of their audit report. And, however serious that may be for the auditors and their professional indemnity insurers, it is not, I think, out of line with public opinion or at least business opinion whose instinctive reaction when an error of an accounting nature comes to light is to ask 'Where were the auditors?'.

And I would think, although the matter has not been judicially tested, the courts — in apportioning liability for a claim arising from an accounting mis-statement — might well be inclined to attach a higher duty of skill and care and consequently a heavier measure of liability on auditors on the ground that accountancy is their business while the business of the directors is to manage the company, in which context the obligation to maintain records and produce accounts is ancillary. And this likelihood will be increased the more complicated and sophisticated accountancy techniques become.

It would be wrong to leave the subject of the sanctions available to ensure that the auditor does his job without a mention of self-regulation. Professional misconduct by an auditor can, of course, result in disciplinary proceedings by his professional body. And this disciplinary sanction can now be extended to apparent failures by members of the accountancy bodies to observe accounting standards or to disclose departures therefrom. I am not aware, however, of any case where disciplinary action has been taken in such a case but it does represent the only effective sanction to secure observance of standards. It means that the auditor may at times have to steer a very narrow course between the Scylla of a rupture of his relations with his clients, which would result from a public disclosure of a disagreement on the appropriateness of a standard, and the Charybdis of disciplinary proceedings in consequence of failure to observe a standard or to disclose a departure from it.

As a lawyer I have a somewhat ambivalent attitude to self-regulation. The case in its favour was eloquently and persuasively put by Lord Shawcross:

> At a time when existing institutions and arrangements are under attack, often for no better reason than that they are existing and so regarded as part of an 'establishment' which should be destroyed, it is right to emphasise the high degree of success which self-regulation and discipline have achieved in this field.
>
> In whatever field of activity, statutory regulations administered by legal authorities can, at the best, lay down no more than minimum standards of behaviour. The danger always is that once such standards are established as rules of law, they come to be regarded as the maximum of what is required and the lawyers (of whom I was one) exercise their ingenuity in finding, as they are entitled to do, ways of avoiding or bypassing the application of the legal rules. Moreover, there is a necessary rigidity in legal rules, a time lag — often very considerable — in adapting

them to new circumstances and a tendency to bureaucratisation (if such a word exists) in their administration.

In this country the statute law as enacted by Parliament does of course apply to very many aspects of company activity, including mergers and take-overs. But what is regarded as good ethical practice has in this field gone far ahead of what Parliament has or indeed ever could lay down. It may indeed be said as a general proposition that where the aim is to establish high standards of conduct in technical or professional matters, the only way in which the maximum standards can be obtained is by self-regulation and discipline. Certainly in regard to take-overs and mergers it is the fact not only that many of the abuses which occurred before the formation of the City Panel could not in practice have been avoided by statutory regulation but that since the Panel asserted its discipline they have, for the most part, ceased to exist. And this in spite of the allegation which is often made that the Panel lacks 'teeth'.[31]

Against that view I put the whole basis of the rule of law; namely, that the law is the measure of legal rights and responsibilities. And by the law I mean a series of definite ascertainable rules which will be applied in accordance with their terms. There is no question of observance in the spirit as well as the letter as the City Code suggests.

The system with its pursuer and defender or prosecutor and accused may be ponderous and unduly formalised but by and large it gives everyone a fair run.

I confess to being uneasy about a system where those who have made the rules are not only the agency for their enforcement but also the judges who decide whether there has been a breach of them. And again the natural desire to show that they have teeth and that self-regulation works produces a danger of over-kill when criticism affecting for example the fitness of a director to continue to act or reflecting on the competence of professional advisers both of a highly damaging character can be made without perhaps the evidence disclosed by their investigators being sufficient to support it.

It is perhaps, like so many things, a matter of balance.

One final word. In May 1976, Lord Justice Scarman addressed the annual conference of the Law Society of Scotland at Aviemore on the subject of 'The Lawyer's Contribution to the Social Revolution'.[32] He made a plea for lawyers if they were going to keep pace with the social revolution, to extend and develop their function in society without losing the respect which they presently enjoyed. We were not to be put off by the danger of becoming involved in political controversy. 'So important is the task', said Lord Justice Scarman, 'that we must run the risk of a stain or two on our beautiful white gown in order that we can do a job of work. I think a little mud on the hands is not always a sign of a misspent life'. Need I spell out the relevance of these remarks to the situation in which the accountancy profession presently finds itself.

NOTES

1. Gower's *Modern Company Law* (third edition) p. 104.
2. *Trevor v. Whitworth* [1887], 12 AC 409, p. 415.
3. Gower, p. 116.
4. Report of the Committee of Inquiry on Industrial Democracy, Cmnd. 6706, p. 60, paras. 8 and 9.
5. Report of the Inflation Accounting Committee (Sandilands Report), Cmnd. 6225, p. 44, para. 153.
6. Gower, p. 549.
7. Sandilands Report, p. 44, para. 154.
8. *The Corporate Report*, a Discussion Paper published for comment by the Accounting Standards Steering Committee (1975).
9. *Aims and Scope of Company Reports*, a preliminary draft paper prepared by the Department of Trade in May 1976 and circulated on an informal basis.
10. *New Brunswick and Canada Railway Land Company* v *Muggeridge* [1860], I Drew and Sm. 363, p. 381.
11. The City Code on Take-overs and Mergers issued on the authority of the City Working Party (1976 Revision).
12. Report of the Company Law Committee, Cmnd, 1749, p. 129, para. 332.
13. Sandilands Report, p. 15, paras. 52 and 53.
14. *Ibid.*, p. 62, para. 231.
15. Statements of Standard Accounting Practice: Explanatory Foreword issued by the Councils of The Institutes of Chartered Accountants of Scotland, in England and Wales and in Ireland, of the Association of Certified Accountants, the Institute of Cost and Management Accountants and of the Chartered Institute of Public Finance and Accountancy.
16. Sandilands Report, p. 165, para. 547.
17. Palmer's *Company Law* (22nd edition), p. 736.
18. *The Accountant's Magazine*, March 1977, Vol LXXXI, No. 849, page 95.
19. Gower, p. 471.
20. Lindley, *L. J. in Re London and General Bank* (No 2) [1895] 2 ch 673, p. 683.
21. Palmer, p. 768.
22. Gower, p. 468.
23. Lopez, *L. J. in Re Kingston Cotton Mill Co.* (No 2) [1896] 2 ch. 279, p. 288.
24. *Fomento (Sterling Area) Ltd.* v. *Selsdon Fountain Pen Co., Ltd, et al* (1958), 1 WLR 45, p. 61.
25. *The Accountant's Magazine*, January 1977, Vol LXXXI, No 847, p. 10.
26. *Ibid.*, p. 13.
27. Gower, p. 468.
28. Shaw. *Accountant's Magazine*, LXXXI, p. 13.
29. *In Re Kingston Cotton Mill Co.* (No 2) [1896] 2 ch. 279.
30. *Hedley Byrne and Co., Ltd.* v. *Heller and Partners, Ltd.* (1963), 2 ALL ER 575.
31. The Panel on Take-overs and Mergers: Report on the Year ended 31 March 1974.
32. *Journal of The Law Society of Scotland*, August 1976, Vol. 21, p. 273.